THE PUBLIC DOMAIN PUBLISHING BIBLE

I0157420

THE PUBLIC DOMAIN PUBLISHING BIBLE

HOW TO CREATE "ROYALTY" INCOME FOR LIFE

ANDRAS M. NAGY

NEW UPDATED EDITION(2024)

Fourth Edition

Murine Publications (2011, 2019, 2024)

ISBN: 978-0-9824994-1-2

Contents

"..Your book is great, and has a lot of useful information, both for people who are "would-be" publishers, and those simply looking to make some money online. Your SEO descriptions are in simple, easy to understand terms, unlike some others I've read and had no clue what they were talking about. Dennise Gubbard

" The Congress shall have the Power..To promote the Progress of Science and Useful Arts, by securing for limited Times to Authors and Inventors the exclusive Right to their respective Writings and Discoveries."(Article I, section 8, clause 8) (From the US Constitution)

Nothing in this book should be construed as legal advice. I am a publisher and not a lawyer. Please, consult your attorney before proceeding with any advice from this book.

Foreword

Even though conventional wisdom suggests otherwise, creative people can copy other people's work and it is legal. How is this possible? By using the vast pool of creative works that fall into a category called Public Domain.

Not everyone can conjure up an original best seller. This book is for those who love books and the literary world but would rather publish other people's masterpieces than labor on their own.

Authors and creative professionals will no doubt find this book of use as well. The cornerstone of using public domain information is to creatively build upon existing ideas and works of art.

With some fresh ideas, and using this book, anyone can do what I have done on a shoestring. There are many aspiring authors who find it comforting to run a publishing company while working on their own creative literary urges. Finding an agent or getting a book published by an unknown author is a major challenge, (I am not talking about vanity presses or self published works but major publishers who can guarantee bookstore presence). Having a publishing background and company can be the only hope to those who wish to see their books published.

The title of the book has the word Bible in it. This paradoxically suggests that I will herein show you my way. What is written here however is not set in stone; it can be subject to interpretation as it is with the "good book" itself.

This book is primarily for public domain titles but assumes that the reader is endowed with some creative value adding talent or aspiration such as writing or illustration because these skills will take you a long way to creating a professional and marketable product. Writing, marketing and selling your own book is especially satisfying while you have some income from old classic reprint books.

We as publishers make money from the difference between the printing cost and the price we set our books at wholesale, times the number of books sold. Royalty or profit, who is to quibble? To me it is all the same, money in the bank, month after month.

I am neither a copyright lawyer nor a legal expert in publishing. I am a publisher with a successful publishing business that I run in my part time, while holding a full time job and raising a daughter. No information in this book is intended to imply that this is an easy business that will alleviate having a job or will make the reader rich. This is, however a business that requires very little start-up cost and no full time involvement.

What is required are: patience, smart, (not hard) work, and perseverance. I have included some web site information with the notion that the world of the Internet is in ever changing flux. Websites and web groups I have listed in this book might not exist anymore. Do not fret, use common sense and Google search to find the ones that undoubtedly replaced those that no longer exist.

I am an amateur writer who had previously used ghost writers. This book is my fifth, and this book is proof that typesetting and style can be learned as well as English grammar and style. However Public Domain publishing requires neither, as the reader can use Word documents and some free or inexpensive PDF creating tools to be a re-print publisher or master writer.

Dover Publications started from the humble Public Domain beginning in 1941 into a full service publishing house. Who knows? Maybe you can do the same!

Why I Wrote This Book

I do not believe in suppressing information. While people warned me not to write and publish this book, I chose to ignore their advice. This book depicts what I do and I wholeheartedly believe in sharing information.

Public Domain publishing is a competitive venue. In my opinion, to launch successfully requires selecting a genre that the publisher must be thoroughly familiar with and deeply love.

In my opinion not all genres of Public Domain works can be sold successfully. This book will explain how the reader can take Public Domain information and create his own unique material. Rare, out of print books could also be included in your publishing repertoire, once the reader is familiar and comfortable with the publishing business and evaluating the antiquarian marketplace.

You must be at your guard at all times, as people will take legal potshots at you. For example there was a New York publisher who had published a book containing only blank pages, and subsequently he was sued by a European blank page publisher. The case was, of course thrown out of the courts as the judge ruled blankness is in the public domain. (From The Joy of Publishing page 159)

This is a business that can generate monthly income without spending too much time away from other pursuits and your family. (A self-publishing couple published a book titled Everything Men Know about Woman. It too was all blank pages. It sold over half a million copies!) The other side of the coin is that your publishing business will not happen overnight. You must 'plant the seed', labor at it slowly and monitor your progress. It is likely that you will not make full-time income from self-publishing for quite sometime.

The way I got involved with self publishing is an interesting story. I wrote white papers and booklets for investment and trading related subjects. I had a consulting business for speculators and traders, mainly focusing on computerized trading, risk management and low impact (read low risk) trading.

My publications while sufficient as stand alone products were the first steps to getting new clients for "time and material" consulting.

I previously used Kinko's copy centers to print and bind my training manuals and sold them via my web site. Needless to say, this process was time consuming, frustrating, and lots of work. Not being satisfied with Kinko's printing, binding and high costs, I was constantly on the prowl for some other solutions. After I closed my consulting business, I was left with years of research material and writing on the subject of trading and risk management. I decided that was just too much hard work to throw away. My own spiritual awakening, and putting my finance and consulting background on hold, lead me to Public Domain works.

I have set up a publishing business that mainly focused on Public Domain works but included my own writings as well. This is how I slowly started to learn about the ins and outs of Public Domain and Print on Demand Publishing. My progress was slow and trial by error. I have made many mistakes that hopefully this book will minimize and perhaps alleviate entirely for my readers. While the concepts of this book have been around for a while, the details and technologies of on demand publishing is an ever changing field. Please keep this in mind.

I. Public Domain in the USA

The US Public Domain law grants authors (and here we are using a broad brush to include all creative endeavors, including writers) exclusive rights to market, publish and sell their work. After this copyright expires and is not extended by the estate of the original copyright holder, the copyrighted work shall fall into the great pool of Public Domain works.

The purpose of this is obvious; it seeks to enhance creative effort by a background of existing art that new artists can build upon. In other words it limits monopoly of thought.

A good example of this is Shakespeare's Romeo and Juliet and the musical West Side Story. Clearly, pundits have drawn the similarities of the story line, yet who can claim that the creator of the West Side Story 'stole' from Shakespeare?

If the date of a book's first publishing was before 1923, it is in the Public Domain. This is a general guideline only; I suggest always having this information verified by a copyright search. In other words, if the work is published, the 1923 date applies; on the other hand unpublished works are under federal copyright for at least the life of the author plus 70 years. (see the line item below)

United States Life + 70 years until year end (works published since 1978 or unpublished works) 17 U.S.C. § 302(a) and 17 U.S.C. § 305 There are countless web sites and forums on Public Domain. Since this is a legal issue, I cannot say a great deal about the legal aspects and angles of this. Laws also change and by the time I publish this book some laws stated herein might become obsolete. Writing this book I wish to put things in print that are not in the state of flux, hence the following list to use as criteria with any book in question:

You must find out...

The date when the work was created.

The date when (or if) the work was registered with the US Copyright Office.

The date when the work was first published.

The country where the work was first published.

Was the work published with a valid copyright notice?

When (or if) the work's copyright was renewed.

If the book is translated from another language, the translations date and lifespan of translator must be considered. If the book is not copyrighted and was published after 1923 it is not public domain because the right is inherent and implied, and falls on the author.

With the passage of the Sonny Bono Copyright Term Extension Act, these works are granted copyright protection for a term ending 70 years after the death of the author. If the work was a work for hire (e.g., those created by a corporation) then copyright persists for 120 years after creation or 95 years after publication, whichever is shorter.

The Stanford University has a copyright renewal database where anyone can search for a status of a book, provided the title and author's name is provided.(http://collections.stanford.edu/copyrightrenewals/bin/page?forward=home)

Since a lot of books were never officially copyrighted it is up to the claimant to prove owner ship and successful registration of a copyright.

Copyright Bullies.

Believe it or not, when money is involved there are always those who will take a cheap shot and try to bully and push around the small business person. Another example of my publishing experience occurred months after I published Manly Palmer Hall's magnum opus "Secret Teachings of All Ages." I received an email from a paralegal working for the Philosophical Research Society, who is legal owner of some of Manly Palmer Hall's books. Since the book is available online, a strong indication of the Public Domain status, I replied to the e-mail sender that I had firmly believed that, according to the US Public Domain Laws, I had every right to publish or alter the book in question. I have never heard a peep from them again.

You see, if there is strong evidence that you have published a book that is not Public Domain and in fact the rights are owned by somebody, then it is prudent action to cease publishing the book and move onto your next project. Honest mistakes happen and there is seldom any further complication from the other party. However, if for some reason you run into someone I categorize as a "copyright bully", you should always do your homework and firmly stand your ground.

I recommend keeping your correspondence written and ask for proof of legal ownership before you roll over to any claimant. The burden of proof is on the claimant where books published long ago are concerned. People who have strong reason to claim copyrights will undoubtedly never email you via paralegal assistants. The claim will come via registered letter.

Copyright Lapsing Let us look at an example; the above mentioned work, "The Secret Teachings of All Ages" written by Manly Palmer Hall and published in the year of 1928 shows, in fact, all the indication of a lapsed copyright status.

The law states that all books published between the years 1923-1962 (inclusive) had to be renewed at the US Copyright Office in the 28th year. If this renewal actually took place, it had to be done between 1955 through 1957.

By searching the website www.ibiblio.com would show this renewal.

This web-page lists all works properly renewed at the US Copyright Office for the year 1928, collated by year of publication and sorted by title. This page relates to books whose titles begin with the letters S through T

These renewals were published in the copyright renewal register during the years 1955-7. The following is the listings under the word 'Secret'. If "The Secret Teachings of All Ages" was renewed properly, it would have been listed following 'The Secret Brotherhood, below;

The Treasure Trove of the US Government

With the freedom of information act, more and more previously secret documents are being released on a myriads of US Government webs-sites. All material is free to use and alter. Believe me most of the publications must be reformatted and rewritten to be of any commercially use but the core it there and it is FREE!

I am not going to list all the extensive subjects and websites here because you have your own initiative and the access. Use it!

Book Covers under Copyright

The other problem I ran into came from laziness rather than carelessness. I have found a real gem of a book, allegedly read by Bill Gates himself, before it prompted him to drop out of Harvard. The book was, without question, free from copyright restriction, but the cover was not!

Instead of designing a great new cover, I decided to use the original in an attempt to recreate ambiance since the book sold large volumes. Needless to say I got a copyright infringement letter from the other party.

This little episode of my publishing career brings us into the areas of other Public Domain works. While this book focuses on publishing books, and everything related to books, it behooves us to know that Public Domain works are available in photography, art (like paintings and drawings), and music and so on.

Librivox has Public Domain books read and recorded as audio recordings. They are a volunteer organization who dedicates their efforts to have great written works on audio, presumably for the reading challenged or sight challenged.

They keep the audio books free of charge and free of copyright. Yes, anyone can use their recordings as they see fit.

Written Copyright Reports

Copyright searches can be done by specialty search firms, publishers and attorneys who specialize in copyright law. You can also go directly to the Copyright Office (CO) and request a copyright search. Further you can request to have it certified by the CO staff. As we discussed above, you could search online, but the results are not as accurate as having the Copyright Office perform this for you. Your own online search should not be used as a definitive answer to your copyright question, but only as a guide. This is the link:

http://www.copyright.gov/records/cohd.html

My personal preference is to use the online search as a general guide and then, if it appears your candidate is in the Public Domain, to get a private search firm or the Copyright Office to conduct a search as well. The important thing to remember is that if you're going to use the work in your own publishing venture, make sure you get a written copyright report from a professional.

If you are not located near the Copyright Office you can follow the instructions below, order your searches by phone or mail and have your Written Copyright Report sent directly to your address.

Upon request, the Copyright Office staff will search its records at the rate of $150 per hour. (This was at the time of writing of this book and maybe inaccurate)

The first step in getting the work you have certified is putting together as much information as possible about the work. The more detailed information you can provide with your request, the less time-consuming and expensive the search will be. Provide as much of the following information as possible:

The title of the work, with any possible subtitles.

The names of the authors, including possible pseudonyms.

The name of the original copyright owner, if exists.

The approximate year when the work was published or registered.

The type of work involved (book, photograph, etc.).

For a work originally published as a part of a periodical or magazine, the title of the publication and the volume or issue number, to help identify it.

The ISBN, Library of Congress registration number or any other copyright data.

Reference and Bibliography Section, LM-451 Copyright Office Library of Congress Washington, D.C. 20559

Generally, in about six to eight weeks the copyright office will send you a written report about the work you have asked them to do a search on. Alternatively you can hire a private search specialist who may do this job for a lesser rate.

Value Added Reselling

I would like to impress upon you the benefit and advantage of the value added concept for public domain publishing. Typically, the Value Added Reselling (or VAR) is known by its utilization in the electronics industry. I think it works perfectly well for Public Domain publishing. You can take something ready made and available, some of which are well known and movies made based upon them, and you can somehow add value to that by clever editorials, footnotes or illustrations. Yes, it is a little more work or more up-front investment but it will pay off in the long run. For example there is a book that is brilliant but it is hard to understand and follow for a variety of reasons. Well, if you know about the subject, you can footnote the content; hence make it more easily understandable for your buyers.

I am sure you have seen slick Internet marketers selling courses and information on Public Domain. What they do not tell you is that the package of information is often full of inaccuracies and errors. For example, one newsletter suggests that anyone can take Public Domain information, simply change it and register it as a new, copyrighted work. The problem is that depending on the extent of the changes, your new copyright in fact might be in error.

Use your own common sense and business acumen. There is a gold mine of free information out there. With the right idea, editorials and creativity you can build a business from the ground up that can augment your earnings, social security and other retirement income.

Appendix A, of this book has some useful web sites to provide Public Domain books and other works potentially useful for the creative publisher.

Public Domain in Other Countries

In general, the Universal Copyright Convention specifies that copyright should run for the life of the author plus at least 25 years which is, in theory long enough time to protect a work during the lifetime of the author and the author's children for their earlier years, should the author die.

Signatories of several international treaties resulted in the extension of the basic, 25-years.

The foremost difference in determining foreign copyright status is first finding the name of the author or authors. Certain works, perfectly usable for reprint, were originated by a corporation or the author is anonymous.

Most countries are more liberal than the US in terms of copyright. The Little Prince is public domain all over the world except in the USA, France and Spain. So if you live in New Zealand, you can reprint and publish this timeless gem.

For example if the book in the Public Domain in all countries except the USA, France and Spain, then even as a US based publisher you can publish and sell these books worldwide with the exclusion of the countries mentioned.

II. How to Select a Genre

Self publishing, as I recommend it, is not for authors with just one book. The business presupposes that you have a number of books and will in fact keep adding new books to your publishing business. Self-publishing is not cost effective for authors who labor on one book for 5 years.

Traditionally, books about the following subjects will be well received:

- Security
- Sex
- Power
- Immortality
- Wealth
- Happiness
- Safety
- Health
- Recognition
- Love

I suggest that your book deliver any of these essential topics. As you see, for Public Domain books, selecting a genre is quite important. Genres available in the Public Domain, while still catering to the palate of the modern reader are not easy to find. As styles of writing differ and can render any book to obsolescence, based on lifestyle and technology. For example, even a well written I suggest that your book delivers any of these essential topics.

Public Domain book on designing of typewriters is of questionable value, except for historical purposes. Of course it can be of some value to collectors and hobbyists but then the book might need to be rewritten if it was originally written to the technical or manufacturing market.

If you are a photographer, you can publish your own collection of photos in addition to having some great Public Domain photo collections in your repertoire.

It is hard for me to impress upon the reader adequately the need for dedication and love towards the genre of your choice. If you wish to publish Classical literary works, you should be reading and studying your genre. If you like poetry, perhaps that genre is to be tried first. Musicians and music lovers can publish Public Domain sheet music for teachers and the musical student market. The reemergence of certain genres can make or break your publishing venue.

Children's Story Writers Those authors who wish to write or publish books for children are in luck as all the famous fairy tales from the Grimm Brothers, L. Frank Baum, to Hans Christian Andersen are in Public Domain. Self publishing these titles maynot work however, and it is easy to see why. Children and parents are impulse buyers and they infrequently order from Amazon.

From my own experience, as a father of a young daughter, megastores always got my book business for my daughter, as patience and waiting for shipping is not something children do well.

"Classics for Young People" (http://www.ucalgary.ca/~dkBrown/storclas.html)is a web based data base by the University of Calgary, including the entire text of the included works such as, The Wizard of Oz.

If you choose to publish classic fairly tales, or children books in Public Domain, usually the original illustrations must be replaced and it is an added cost consideration. Later in this book I mention cost effective ways of hiring free-lancers and copy editors.

Chess Books

Any games published before 1923 which have not renewed their copyright are subject to being republished by any chess aficionado, especially if comments are written, offering a fresh look at some timeless games.

http://www.chessgames.com is a free, searchable database with one search criteria being a date.

I have placed 'no later than 1923' into the date field, clicked 'with kibitzing' and 'with annotation' fields and clicked on the 'Find Chess Games' button - 614 games resulted in my search.

Cookbooks

If you are a culinary expert or just a kitchen hobbyist this genre can make you a success.

Public Domain cookbooks and recipe collections can be a true gold mine! If you go a little further, and after trying out each and every one of the recipes you take some good pictures of the resulting dishes, Bingo! You now have a semi private copyrightable creation that is based on a legal use of an existing work. To avoid liability issues stemming from possibly offering unhealthy dishes, you can adjust the recipes to suggest the reader replace unhealthy ingredients with appropriate healthful substitutions to appeal to people with health issues and sedentary lifestyles. How would you go about finding out of print cookbooks? As always, the answer is research and more research… I would take a stab at Project Gutenberg first, which is an online resource for e-books.

Here is what I found in a few seconds….

Project Gutenberg: Seventy-Five Receipts for Pastry Cakes and Sweetmeats http://www.gutenberg.org/dirs/etext04/svfvr10.txt

I have also found a site with a long list of used and out-of-print cookbooks that are for sale. You might look through the list and see if anything strikes your fancy and have some of them scanned. http://www.foodbooks.com/used_cookbooks.htm

Military/survival books and CIA publications

The United States government and its agencies have a wealth of information published as field manuals or declassified documents.

Esoteric and New Age

I was very lucky. I chose New Age and spirituality as my genre because I went through a spiritual transformation and begun studying the subject in depth.

Spirituality is a growth business today. When Oprah Winfrey publicly endorsed new age authors, they, effectively became "gurus". While I personally find this laughable, it depicts the current state of affairs, and the thirst and vacuum organized religion left behind.

But, that is enough about my selection of genre. You must somehow do the same and a well chosen market segment will make or break you.

I must warn you do not just pick a genre because it is perceived to be popular. Do it because you believe in it and love it. This is the very reason I decided to go ahead and write this book. Sure, people can attempt to copy my business, and replicate what I have written. Yes, they can fake their enthusiasms and zeal for the subject matter. But that will last only a few weeks or months.

Write a Screenplay based on a Public Domain novel.

Writing a screenplay takes lots of work and dedication. (I only recommend using screen writing in addition to building a publishing business.

This is not for everybody but the dreamer aspirant to the movie business.) When you are writing anything you always have a set of requirements that you need to meet in order to make it an effective piece of writing. Don't let that discourage you however, there are a

few ways that you can make your ventures into screen writing a lot
easier than you would have expected it to be. In fact, pretty much
everyone can start producing their own screenplay easily.

First of all, understanding what a screenplay is exactly is a good
start to figuring out what you are going to write, or how you are
going to write. When you are writing a regular story, that is something people are going to read and imagine exists, it is completely
different when you are writing a script.

You are going to write dialogs, sounds, and picture elements.
You are probably going to imagine throughout your writing what
visuals are going on, but when your script goes into production, all
the people involved (directors, actors, producers, etc.) are going to
want to have their own artistic say in your story.

So when you are writing, going into huge detail on visual
elements may just be involving more work for you that might be
changed later on, so you are going to concentrate on major elements, like a story line. When you are a writer, trying to find things
to write about is probably one of the hardest things you need to
come up with. Not only does it be an idea of something people
want to go see, but you need to know some twists and turns in your
story to make people stay engaged throughout your presentation.

You can approach screen writing ideas from many different
vantage points. You can think up things that have happened to you
in the past and write about them, you can ask friends for interesting
stories you might elaborate into a tale, you can scour the boundaries
of your imagination for an interesting and fresh idea.

You might have already taken a course on screenplay writing.
These are excellent for giving you a foundation in screenplay writing
and formatting for screenplays. Courses range from a few hours
in one day to a few hours a week over several months. If you are
looking into taking a course, you want one where there aren't a huge
number of students, and that encourages you to submit different
works of your writing for evaluation.

When you take a course you want to get to know your teacher,
so he or she is giving you crucial feedback on your projects. When
you do get feedback, accept it for good advice. Even if it feels like a
personal attack, it likely isn't, and you don't have to make changes
other people suggest. It is hard to take criticism when writing can
be a very emotional journey.

If you have or haven't taken a course, then you might want to
look into screenplay software available through the internet. Some
software packages just include formatting capabilities others offer
features that will assist you in writing or adapting plays.

There is a common way many people break into screen writing without the added pressure of determining all the plot details of their screenplays. Have you ever watched the movie Dracula?

There are so many different versions out do you remember which version it was? Was it a made for TV movie? Was it a low key/low budget production? Was it one that had a lot of famous people in it? There are so many different movies out there based on Dracula, or with Dracula in the title it is almost an epidemic. You would think that people would not be able to create so many films without the acceptance of the author, and how can they get that if he is dead?

Well here is when you hear about the trick of using public domain works. These are books, or even movies and other works of art that are not under any copy write protection so therefore free for you to use. What does this mean for someone who wants to write a screenplay? Well you are entitled to read these books, and you are able to adapt them as you see fit!

You are entitled to use the ideas that come up in these works for your own purposes. You can stay absolutely true to the storyline, which may be hard because books written for reading don't always have the acting thought out of certain situations, or you can adapt it. When you are a beginning writer, this technique has a lot of advantages because it is like having someone there to back you up every step of the way.

There are a few different places you can go to find these works. You can visit a library and ask a librarian for assistance with books they know to be entered into the public domain, or you can do online searches for public domain books. Many websites are out there and have converted public domain books into e-books that are free for you to download and adapt as you wish. You will probably come across many classics that you remember reading as you grew up.

When it comes to selecting the book, you have a wide range of options. Dracula, as mentioned above is a very popular book to adapt. Many of Shakespeare's plays have also gone through overhauls, especially the popular Romeo and Juliet. You want a book that appeals to you because: if you like it chances are good that other people like it too, and if you enjoy reading it, you will probably get great enjoyment out of adapting it for the screen.

One area that is known especially for creating screenplays from the public works domains is works from children's literature, who hasn't heard of Alice in Wonderland. These types of screenplays are loved by both adults and children.

No matter what topic you decide on, you do want to ensure that you aren't crowding the market on an already rehashed story. You also want to consider your best style of writing and the market you want to appeal to with a finished product. As long as it is a topic that interests you, your enthusiasm is going to appeal to those you want to sell it to.

Should you decide you are going to adapt an existing public domain book into a screenplay, here are some tips for performing this: You will need to read the piece you have selected several times. Generally you are going to have chosen a book from the public domain, but who knows, you might come across a piece of poetry that has inspired you. The more you know about the characters and story lines in your selection, the easier your own adaptation will be to write. When you get to know a story so well you can read it without looking at the written words, then you can take it and start making adaptations in your imagination before writing them down. Work on what you need to include in your screenplay. The book might have taken you 20 plus hours to read, but no one is going to sit in any theatre for 20 plus hours watching the whole story in great detail. What you want to do is keep the main points of the story in your screenplay and whittle down the rest.

If there are characters that do not have significance in the movie, then write them out. People want to go to a movie or play and see drama, what are the most dramatic or moving parts of the story, make sure you keep those in the final draft. You will want to pay attention to time periods of the novel, and time periods of today. If your adaptation is more current to today's time frame then you need to ensure the parts of your screenplay are updated to reflect the current population. This would be more common when you are adapting old English stories, if you can manage to read one, then you need to understand it and not use any old fashioned wording in it or your audience will just be confused. When it comes to writing from books, you need one that has a lot of narrative elements in it.

If, after reading through your book you find it has a majority of thematic representations, or is highly literary, it is going to be very difficult to translate into a screenplay. If, after you have read through the book, and are trying very hard to extract a visual representation of most of the main elements of the story, you might be better off to put that book back and try another one. After you have chosen your book and have started writing your screenplay. You want to pay attention to the important elements of screenplay writing. You can find several websites that are devoted to helping you correctly format your finished work. The guidelines on screenplay formatting are pretty strict, so here is where you get your money out of the software system you invested in. When you are writing your script you want to keep the intended market in mind, you want to pay attention to length, particularly if you are writing for a short television show. Traditionally a script for a feature film will be between 90 to 130 pages long. Keep in mind, it may take you a few seconds to read something, but if people need to act it out, it can take much longer. If you have written a script that is pretty long and you try to take it to someone for a read through, they may just look at the number of pages and dismiss your work right away as too long. Make sure then that you are erring on the side of too short. This brings us to marketing your script. Nobody wants to go through all the effort of writing a screenplay to have it sit on your shelf!

Finding a buyer for your script is probably the most difficult part of screenplay writing, next to coming up with a fresh idea! First you want to think of people you know in the business. It is always easier to sell something when you have a foot in the door already. Contact anyone who you know is even remotely in the business. Telling people you have a screenplay ready might just hit the right ears. If you don't have any connections, it is going to be harder. When you have your script in hand, you want to ensure that you have a very professional script, that you have tended to all the little things that are needed in a script, that it is complete, and you have proofread it several times for errors. If you don't take the time to do this, then why would someone who has limited time available do it for you? Next, get ready for a lot of "No".

You don't need to have metal shell around you, you want to remain on friendly terms, but you need to recognize that you are going to get a lot of "no's" even when you haven't shown your masterpiece to anyone yet. Just remember every no, is a step closer to a yes. Contact agencies that are open to new talent. You can write many of the major agencies, but it is likely you will get a polite no thank-you letter back. What you need to do is keep on. Write to all the agencies you can think of, and send them a short outline of your script. Eventually you will come across someone who is interested, and suddenly, you become officially a screenwriter! Screen writing can be a difficult business, but if you have solid writing skills, and an aptitude for converting novels to screenplays you can carve out a healthy little niche in the marketplace, all it takes is a lot of determination.

III. The Print on Demand Advantage

In the old days of publishing, the publisher had a number of print-ers on contract which supplied the printed books. Those in turn, the publisher sold via wholesale buyers to the bookstores, libraries and other places selling and stocking books.

This business model is still in operation as market paperback books can be printed in volume very cheaply and then the stores will stock them at Borders or Barnes and Noble.

Large, conglomerate bookstore chains will require a right of return to the books for any reason. This means that the publisher must take back books that the retail chain refuses to stock any-more. This obviously can kill a small startup publishing business. When considering the cost of publicity, promotions and market-ing, returns are not acceptable. You as a small publisher must say no to returns.

Barnes and Noble will do business with a select number of small press and independent publishers, but the catch is, they still demand the right of return. I had contemplated applying for this, but to my knowledge either all books or none must be in the agree-ment application. I am apprehensive to this corporate blackmail from big retail stores.

Advent of Print of Demand (POD)

Print on demand publishing does not use offset printing tech-nologies that traditional printers use. POD printers use digital printing which is in a sense replicating the pages from a digital master, usually a PDF document.

Most books printed by traditional publishers and few self-publishers use the offset lithography process. It wasn't too long ago that everyone had considered the quality of offset printing to be vastly superior to digital printing. But all of that has changed. Recent technical advances in digital printing have helped POD printers catch up in quality, although it still may be years before they can match the cost of offset printing.

The Advantage of on Demand Publishing

To fully appreciate this, the reader either had to have been in the often perilous business of traditional publishing, or tried to fabricate a business plan for such a business.

Simply put, traditional printers must have adequate funds to order sometimes five hundred or a thousand books of a title. What happens if the title does not sell? Not only did the publisher have to shell out the original printing costs, but as books were either returned or never got ordered by stores, he is now stuck with a bunch of books. This is dangerous with original titles but especially dangerous with Public Domain book titles otherwise available. Fortunately this is not the case with on demand publishing. There is no up-front cost, no inventory, and if you do it my way, minimal cost.

IV. How to Construct your Book

We have come a long way since the "qwerty" keyboard of the Remington typewriter was replaced by the IBM Selectric and that, in turn has been replaced by the computer based word processor.

Desktop publishing technologies advance by leaps and bounds. Every five years or so there is some new technology that professes to make author's lives easier and more productive. I am still waiting for the perfect word processor that will help me in writing my best seller.

The advent of postscript based document processing propelled Adobe to be the premier provider of desktop publishing software, pushing Microsoft to second fiddle status.

I have worked as a technical writer for the IT industry using Microsoft Word and I firmly believe that using MS Word alone, a publisher can be successful and create professional looking books.

Parts of a Book

Front Matter – A book is divided into three distinct parts. The first part of a book is known as the front matter. The front matter contains pages normally found in every book such as the title page, copyright page, and table of contents. These pages are numbered using roman numerals rather than the more common Arabic numbering. Along with the more common pages are a number of lesser known pages such as the Epigraph Page, Frontispiece, and Half Title Page. View a complete listing of front matter pages, and their function in the book. Our Glossary will also explain the use of each of these parts of a book.

Core Matter – The second part of a book is known as the core matter. The core matter is also referred to as the body of the text. When developing a book layout, these are the pages that require most of the attention in regard to choosing font styles, font size, margin settings, and so on.

Back Matter – The third part of a book is known as the back matter. The back matter contains a number of lesser known pages such as the Epilogue, Afterword, and Glossary. The back matter pages are numbered along with the core matter pages using the Arabic numbering rather than the roman numerals used in the front matter. Many books are produced which do not contain any of the back matter pages.

The need for an index is largely dependent on the book's genre. Historical and Genealogical books often have indexes to help readers track the hundreds of people, places, or events that happen throughout the book. Most books (Novels, Poetry, Art Books, Children's Books) do not require an index. If you feel that by indexing you 'd set your edition apart from other you may want a full index especially if the original edition has it, Re-indexing is easier than setting up the index as initial, since it is likely that page numbers will change.

Adobe is expensive and often unnecessary for manuscript writing. You may decide to purchase Adobe products and there is nothing wrong with that. Just keep in mind that your business success will depend on keeping your startup costs down. The monthly cost of InDesign is relatively low but you could factor in a course in the software use as it is not trivial. Still, using templates such as this book's base will make your book stand out from the myriads of amateurish looking books.

When reading this chapter, the reader should keep in mind that the quality, look and feel of a book published and sold is a reflection on them. This means typesetting, font selection, layout design and more. But content is what makes or breaks a book, not typesetting. The mere look and feel by layout cannot compensate a poorly written and poorly edited manuscript.

Both layout design and content must be of a high standard to be worthy of publishing. Keep in mind that this will not happen overnight. Either you must pay for top notch talent to design your layout and cover, or you must become competent to do the job yourself.

Designing a book gets my creative juices flowing. Even if the book is a Public Domain work that I chose to republish, designing a proper cover can be a very creative and rewarding task.

Some people maintain that professional book design cannot be achieved using Microsoft Word. I happen to agree. You will need to have your book in a digital format. This means either in Adobe Distiller, or Microsoft Word format. If you have found an old, out of print book then you will need to scan it or have someone scan it for you. I have used a scanning service that I found both inexpensive and fast.

The web site is:
http://www.bookscanning.com/index.html

I am sure there are others, so do your due diligence and ask lots of questions.

When I started out in this business I was going out of my way to save a few dollars here and there, while using every tool and web service that was offered for free to my advantage. Even today, I am proud to say, I still do not own Adobe Illustrator a software package many would say is the basic essential for a desktop publisher and book designer. The PDF format, Lighting Source accepts has to meet certain criteria. This is clearly stated in their DigitalFileSubmission. pdf directly accessible from their website.

What does all of that mean? This is why I suggest you only use the free PDF software if you are very adventurous and computer savvy. Here is what I did to save a few dollars, when I started out. I have used Lulu.com to learn the ins and outs of book construction and design. While using Lulu has disadvantages, it is completely free, has a wide variety of book formats and most importantly creates PDF files that are completely acceptable to LSI stringent requirements.

Having used Lulu served me well during the time they had "LiveHelp" chat, an online support feature. This sadly was cut as a cost saving measure while I was still a complete novice on internal book design, cover design and book typesetting in general.

I suggest the reader sticking to one format initially, and use fonts other than what is standard in the Microsoft Word or Adobe InDesign, which is Times New Roman (Times New Roman is completely unsuitable for a book. Georgia and Garamond are better. My favorite is California FB, as this book demonstrates). But in general mainstream publishing these fonts are matching to the genre's listed;

Garamond
Poetry Books
Children's Books
Novels
Biographies
Cookbooks
Yearbooks
Baskerville
Poetry Books
Novels
Biographies
Art Books
Caslon
Poetry Books
Children's Books
Novels

Biographies
Cookbooks
Yearbooks
Font selection is a subtle art of book design, this book is using Minion Pro, so obviously the above is a guideline and not a rule.

Experiment and see what attracts you.

The reader should bear in mind that his profit per book will be around $1.50 to $10, depending on the uniqueness of the book. Spending funds on something not completely necessary will hinder and delay your profitability. I have currently moved up in the world to Adobe Creative suits (subscription model) but for a cover I still use Scirbus which is a open source PDF designer.

I have downloaded and tried OpenOffice suite but I found their user interface cumbersome and not well done. There will be a time when you would like to change the PDF file dimensions.

I do the following:

In Google, I type in; "convert inches to Adobe points". The first result is an online service called

http://www.onlineunitconversion.com/cape.inch_to_point. Adobe.html is a web site where you want to select "inch, International, US" as "from" and "Adobe Points" as "to" size. When you type in 6 inches the result should be 6 inch [international, U.S.] = 432 point [Adobe]. These numbers you will use in PDF Tools to re-size your PDF.

At the writing of this book, the CAD-KAS PDF Editor 2.4 is the only PDF editor that you can use short of leasing(and learning) the Adobe product.

At this point it is uncertain if CAF-KAS PDF Editor would satisfy Lightning Source stringent PDF requirement for the book-block or book cover.

Scribus Open SourceSource Desktop Publishing.

Scribus[1] is an open-source program that brings award-winning professional page layout to Linux/UNIX, Mac OS X, OS/2 and Windows desktops with a combination of "press-ready" output and new approaches to page layout. Underneath the modern and user friendly interface, Scribus supports professional publishing features, such as CMYK color, separations, ICC color management and versatile PDF creation.

It is ideal to use Scribus with Gimp, a free image editing pack-

---

1   This software can be downloaded for free from http://www.scribus. net.

age you can download from http://www.gimp.org/. In order to use any images you must assure that the image is at least 300 DPI. Using Gimp you can easily create higher resolution and you do not need to worry about RGB color space because Adobe Acrobat can automatically convert any color space to the required CMYK.

There are so many PDF and desktop publishing tools for free or for a very low cost that mentioning them all here would derail the scope of this book.

It is no secret that we live in a technological age. The digital revolution has indeed changed the way in which society operates and the way in which we perform everyday tasks. For example, reading has changed exponentially in recent years. Nobody would have ever thought that we would be able to change the way we read twenty years ago but nonetheless a change has occurred. Today, you can pick up a traditional book and begin to read or log on to your computer, select a digital book and do it that way. There are even e Book readers that you can purchase for your digital book copies. However, it is largely thanks to book scanning that all of these changes to the way in which we read could take place.

Book scanning is a relatively new concept that allows books to be copied and made available to millions of people the world over. It is a fantastic way to ensure that people have access to antiquarian books that would otherwise be off limits or left open to damage. However, to understand how old book and book scanning relate to each other, you first have to look into exactly what book scanning is.

What Is Book Scanning? Book scanning is effectively the process that occurs to convert an actual book with physical pages into a digital copy. Each page or set of pages is converted into a digital image and then placed online for individuals to read. This is actually achieved by image scanning, or producing an image of each page, which is obviously a lot less time consuming than typing the entire book out again from the first word to the last word.

The process is a little more complex than simply scanning the pages though, with each page image being re-compiled into a book. All the pages are placed in sequence and reproduced for reading via your computer screen rather than on paper.

There are numerous formats that books are stored in after they have undergone book scanning. Some are stored as a PDF (Portable Document Format) file, .tiff (Tagged Image File Format) file or similar formats that are easily accessible and readable. However, they are a little bulky, which is why software that uses optical character recognition (OCR) is commonly used. OCR is officially the following:

OCR (Optical Character Recognition) is the process of turning a picture of words (such as a scan of a typed letter) into an editable document that you can open and use in your desktop publishing software, word processor, or other text editor.

Not only does it improve the quality of the images but it also reduces the amount of storage needed to keep these books on file. Furthermore, OCR allows reformatting of the text as well as making searching and inputting the text far easier.

So now you know what book scanning is, it is time to find out exactly how it is done, where you can get the end results and how you could do it.

What Methods Of Book Scanning Are Used? There are two main methods of book scanning or at least two broad categories that are used to classify how books are scanned. They are known as destructive scanning and non-destructive scanning.

Destructive book scanning is exactly what the name suggests – destroying the book in order to scan the pages individually. This is the most cost effective way of book scanning but is actually the worst for book loves, and definitely not the way you want to go if you have an antiquarian bookstore and want to reproduce the books whilst keeping the originals intact.

The idea behind traditional book scanning is that the book is removed from its binding and all of the pages are cut into the same dimensions using a larger guillotine cutter. When that is complete, the pages are scanned individually with a regular scanner that has an automatic document feeder (ADF) incorporated into it. However, this is not suitable for books of value so it is important to look for non-destructive book scanning methods.

Non-destructive scanning methods use book scanners and OCR software. There are numerous products on the market that can enable you to do this without causing as much as a crease to one of the pages. It is possible to choose one of two systems for scanning in this way:

Some high-end scanning systems employ vacuum and air and static charges to turn pages while imaging is performed automatically, usually from a high resolution camera located over an adjustable v-shaped cradle.

Both methods can be used to replicate books in the public domain so that the individuals copying them can make money from the content and keep every single penny of the profits in most cases, and there are numerous examples of that available online.

Finding Scanned Books There are numerous sources of scanned books available today, with the vast majority being available online via services like Google Books, Project Guttenberg and the Open Content Alliance. As such, it is relatively easy to find them via search engine. The above are all free to search so all visitors are able to access all of the books on there. However, there is numerous subscription services that give you access to a much wider range of scanned books. Questia and JSTOR are two paid for services that are geared towards students but many universities and colleges offer access to scanned books online for their own students.

The vast majority of the books on Google Books are in the public domain and so not within copyright. As such, they can place the books online without infringing copyrights. Some of the books that do appear on there are not out of copyright but are not excluded on account of other legal clauses.

All of the services named above offer a service that is made possible by large scale scanning of books in much the same way, although some do make royalty payments. However, when it comes to antiquarian books, book scanning can be a useful tool in replicating them for mass distribution without damaging them. If you want to scan books, particularly older and more collectible books that are of value, then you will find that most no longer have copyright laws attached. Public domain material is often available to all without anyone else having a legal claim to the work. When you get around the legal issues this way, all which is left to do is find decent software and services that can scan for you.

OCR Software and Scanners[2]

If you want to create unique, marketable content then you effectively have two options. The first is only suitable if you plan for book scanning to be a one-time effort because it involves hiring a book scanning company to provide you with a copy of the book in question, which you are then of course free to do whatever you like with. This requires the minimum investment because you do not have to purchase the equipment yourself. A scanning company can provide you with quality and faultless copies so literally all you have to do is use the scanned book as you see fit.

However, if you want to make the scanning of public domain antiquarian books a long term project then you should consider setting up an operation of your own because the scanner and OCR software would pay for themselves in an incredibly short period of time. To do that, you need to know the best software and scanners available as well as how to do it yourself.

2   There are a couple of nondestructive book scanners on Amazon as low as $425, I personally would not pay any less for quality concerns,.

There are numerous OCR software packages out there and some scanners even come with their own basic software already installed. However, before you use that then be sure to look at the software your scanner has. Does it fulfill all your wants and needs? Is it easy to use? Is it suitable for professional use? If the answer to any of those questions is no then you should look to find a more comprehensive package.

Adobe Acrobat is of course the primary OCR software for PDFs already available.

There are other comprehensive packages on the market, but there seem to be three in particular that catch the eye of the experts every time: ABBYY FineReader, OmniPage Professional 16, and TypeReader 2008.

ABBYY FineReader is OCR software that has proved popular with researchers who process document after document on a daily basis. The simple tasks that are performed by the software produce fantastic results, removing all fuzzy and unclear elements and ensuring that documents are perfect for reproduction. The Quick-Tasks function is an automated system that can produce various file formats so that you can proof the final copies and ensure that all errors are removed before you use those books in the public domain for your own purposes.OmniPage Professional 16 is much better for you if you want to produce a lot of book scanning material. It does seem initially complex and rather confusing but you will soon see that it is simple to use and produces incredibly high quality when it comes to converting files. The text accuracy is second to none and the features are incredibly powerful. This is recommended for business book scanning so it will suit your purpose if you plan to reproduce plenty of material.

TypeReader 2008 is the third OCR software package but easily the fastest. It was initially designed for corporate use and can scan 700 pages, converting it into an editable document, within 6 minutes. Although not as accurate as the OmniPage Professional 16, it is just as effective providing that you are prepared to proofread.
Of course, there are plenty of other OCR software packages for book scanning out there but you have to weigh up the pros and cons before you buy. A list of possible software packages can be found on the OCR Wiki page.
There is a definite advantage in doing the scanning yourself. The fact that you can control it is important; especially when it comes

to material with a good resell value for you. According to Jacci Howard Bear, there are some essential tips that you should always adhere to when you scan a book, no matter what the scanner and software combination you use:

Begin with the best possible original. You need to ensure that the paper is as flat and even as possible. If the pages are even slightly wrinkled then the light will be drawn to specific elements of the text, which will effectively ruin the scan. Ensure that the pages are flat by using a heavy book or warm iron to smooth them over and remove any smudges as far as possible.

Make sure that the scan is as good as it can possibly be. The scanner bed and glass should be clear and free from debris or smears. You also need to ensure that the document is as straight as possible so that you do not end up with a skewed image of the page as this is difficult to correct. You should experiment with the color, contrast and brightness of the scanner as well to ensure that the background is white. It will also be necessary to make sure that the scanned image is set at 300 dpi or better.

Strip down your document where necessary. For example, if you are scanning an antiquarian book then the likelihood is that it will have various columns and sidebars that newer texts do not tend to have. As such, you should use the software to the best possible effect by scanning each section one at a time. Be sure to use the cropping tools to remove images and other non text material. You may lose a little of the formatting but the most up to date software does allow for the retention of some of the formatting. As such, if you do lose too much, try the upgraded versions of the software.

Make the most of your settings options. There are usually plenty of settings available for you to choose from on your OCR software and scanner so try out some different ones. The more settings you try from the outset, the better your final copies will be.

Proofread the final copy. When you have finished the book scanning, be sure to proof all of the information that is contained within it. You need to ensure that everything is in order because software programs are accurate but not completely 100% reliable. Your eyes are the most reliable tool you have so make the most of them.

All of the above information is designed to give you the best possible start in your quest for book scanning tools. Now you can use book scanning to reproduce public domain books for your own personal use, whether you choose commercial purposes or not. You have to find a system that works for you, although you might like to check out the Google patent to see exactly how they do it and achieve so much in the way of success!

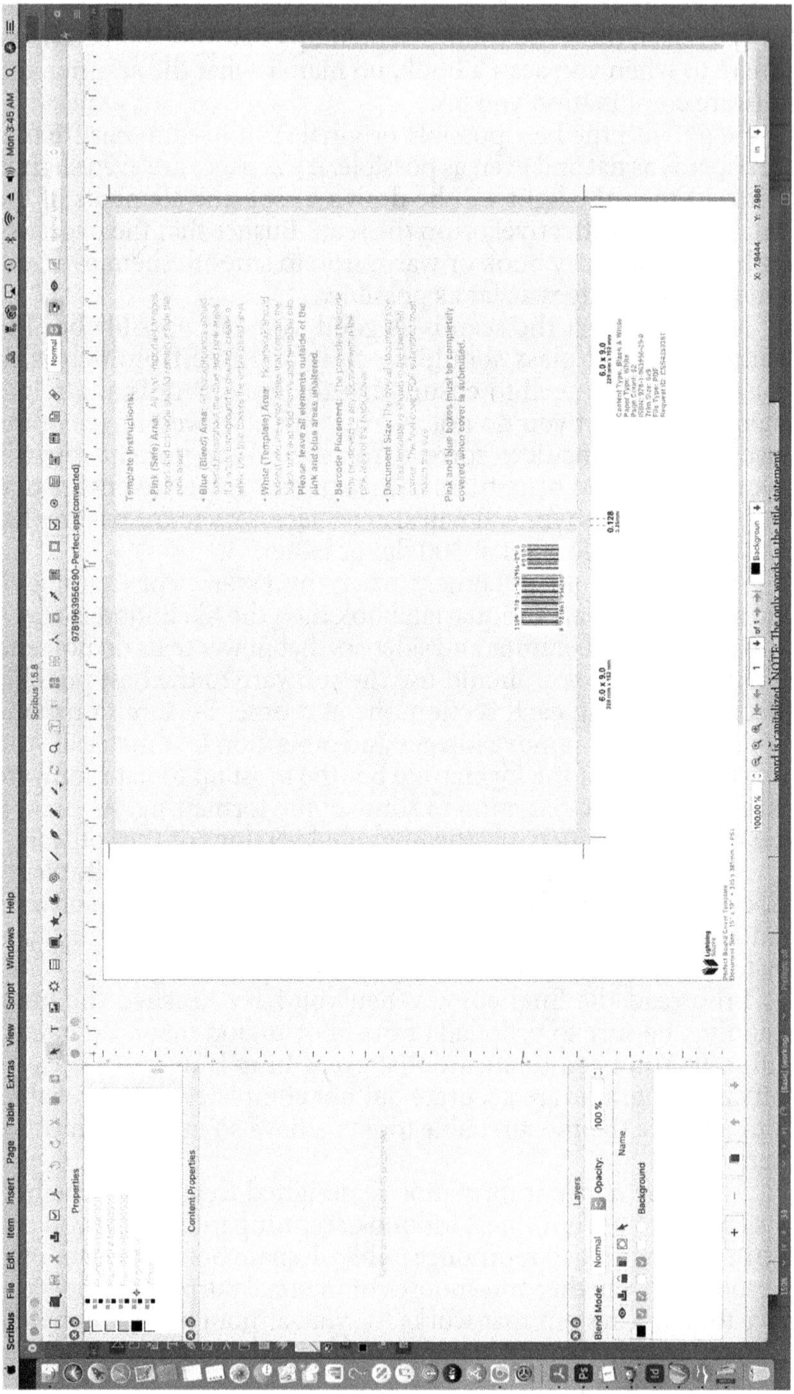
Scribus 1.5.8
9781963956290-Perfect.eps(converted)
Properties
Content Properties
Template Instructions:
Pink and blue boxes must be completely covered when cover is submitted.
6.0 x 9.0
0.128
6.0 x 9.0
Layers
Blend Mode:
Normal
Opacity:
100 %
Name
Background

V. Book Cove Design with Scribus

There is one reprint publisher who has over ten thousand titles and the covers of the books are all the same. Obviously this publisher wants to convey the message and put the emphasis on the printed word. This is fine but in the realm of public domain you will seldom be the only publisher. Sooner or later some other publisher will find out about the marketability of a certain title, purchase that book and scan it. If there is money to be made someone will do it.

What can distinguish your publishing business from the next guy is a smart but not too fancy cover. A cover that conveys the message and the ambiance of the book perfectly – a cover that sells!

A smart looking cover is not too fancy but pleasing to look at with special emphasis in font selection, color and graphics images. Marketing in cyberspace, especially Amazon, you should consider a cover that looks good in small, thumbnail image format as well.

After establishing the ISBN and page size of your book you can request a Cover template online from LSI/Ingram. You'd need to specify the format and dimensions for the book as well as other characteristics such is black and white or colored, matte or gloss, etc.

You can request the template as a PDF or InDesign document. Ask fro a PDF file.

In a minute or two the Template will be mailed to you. When opening the PDF with Adobe Acrobat you can export it as .eps (encapsulated postscript file). That is the format Scribus understands. Open Scribus and read in the eps file. Now you are ready to make your cover. Under the windows tag (F6) will open the layers dialogue. For each element in your cover you ideally should have a layer assigned. The first layer should be ISBN. After created the ISBN layer go back to the basic layer (background) and under Item/grouping/ungroup (CTRL+SHFT+G) - ungroup all the elements in the original layer (including the ISBN), then under Edit/deselect all (CTRL+SHFT+A).

At this point you can select the ISBN field while still remaining in the background. The ISBN has three parts upper lower and whole body. The upper and lower black must be total black[3] thus you must change its properties otherwise LSI/Ingram will reject it.

After you have changed the color black to total black you can individually move the items to the ISBN layer. The other important issue when saving the file as PDF the check box 'convert spot colors

---

3   in Scribus it is called Registration(?)

Munich

THE TRUE STORY OF THE ISRAELI RESPONSE
TO THE 1972 OLYMPIC MASSACRE AND THE
DEVELOPMENT OF INDEPENDENT COVERT ACTION TEAMS

ALEXANDER B. CALAHAN

Israelis and top intelligence officials put pressure on Meir, and he reluctantly gave the go-ahead for the broad assassination campaign to begin. But when West Germany released the three people who were still alive after the massacre a few months later, as the hijackers of Lufthansa Flight 615 had asked, she no longer felt ambivalent. For Israeli intelligence, the committee's first task was to compile a list of all those involved in Munich who warranted death. This was possible with the help of PLO agents working for Mossad and information from European intelligence agencies that were friendly. Reports say that the final number of targets is between 20 and 35, with a mix of Black September and PLO elements. No one knows what's on the whole list. After this was done, Mossad was told to find the people and kill them.

The idea of plausible deniability—that it shouldn't be possible to show a direct link between the killings and Israel—was very important to the planning. The operations also aimed to intimidate Palestinian militants from a wider perspective. David Kimche, who used to be the deputy head of Mossad, said, "The goal wasn't so much revenge as to scare them [the Palestinian terrorists]." It was our goal for them to feel like we were watching them from behind. So, we tried not to do something as simple as shooting a guy in the street. That would have been easy and fair.

VI. How to build a CIP data block

Obtaining an ISBN number and Library of Congress Catalog in Publication (CIP) data block is not mandatory. In this chapter we shall examine the need and usefulness of CIP and the need for Preassigned Control Number (PCN).

What are these numbers you might ask? The CIP and the PCN are numbers to catalog your book so libraries can and would order them. Whether this is something you want or not, will depend on the genre and uniqueness of your book.

Usually people have someone with library science background to create the CIP block for them but in this book you will find out that, with some guidance, you can do the job just as well.

The CIP data block contains your ISBN and CIP number (Pre-assigned Control Number) that you can obtain from the Library of Congress.

Here is this book's CIP data block with some explanations.

Publisher's Cataloging-in-Publication data (1)

Nagy, Andras Miklos (2)

The public domain publishing bible: how to create royalty income for life/(3) written by Andras M. Nagy p.cm (4)

1st Edition (5)

Includes Bibliographical References (6)

Includes Indexing (7)

ISBN 978-0-9824994-1-2 (8)

1. Public Domain. 2. Self-Publishing. 3. Book-Marketing. 4. on-Demand Printing/Publishing. 5. Copyright USA (9)

Z278-549 (10) 2009933517 (11)

(1) Publisher's Cataloging-in-Publication Data. This tells the librarian that it is a CIP block supplied by the publisher.

(2) This is called the Main Entry. Typically it is the author's name and it is one way in which the book is indexed in the Library of Congress's catalog. (3) Title statement. Notice that only the first word is capitalized. NOTE: The only words in the title statement that are capitalized are the first word and any proper names in the statement.

(4) Statement of responsibility. This is written exactly as it appears on your title page. (5) This is the physical description of the book, but it's typically left blank. I don't know why! Once librarians have the book in hand they may fill in these details themselves.

(6) Statement of index and/or bibliographic references. (7)

International Standard Book Number. If the book has an ISBN 13 or two ISBNs (one for hardcover and one for paperback, for example) they will both go here. You need an ISBN if you want to sell your book through bookstores or distribute to libraries. You can get a block of them through R.R. Bowker.

(8) Subject headings. These are chosen based on authority records already in the Library of Congress database. NOTE: They cannot be made up and you cannot include records that don't already exist!

(9) Additional entries. This means other ways your title will be inputted into the library's databases. In addition to author, it will be inputted by title. It could also be inputted through a second author's name, if that applies.

(10) Library of Congress classification number. In this case it puts the book next to other books on library science, book selling and publishing. This classification is used by university libraries and other large library systems.

(11) This is the PCN (Preassigned Card Number) or LCCN (Library of Congress Control Number). If you rather have someone do this for you. I can highly recommend a person who inspired this chapter of the book via her web site (http://www.cipblock.com/) and services she provides to the publishing community. Her name is Adrienne Ehlert Bashista. The last time I worked with her she charged $50 for one CIP data block.

The Library of Congress Control Number is a 12 digit number issue by the Library of Congress to give basic cataloging information to libraries and bookstores. Residents of the United States are able to apply for a Library of Congress Control Number (LCCN). There is currently no charge for this service. To obtain a Library of Congress Control Number, please visit LOC.gov to create an account and register.

The vast majority of reprint books do not consider the LCCN to be a priority. As a result, most self-published books do not contain the Library of Congress Control Number.

VII. How to Work with Lightning Source or Ingram Spark

To become a bona fide on demand publisher you must eventually open a LightningSource.com (will refer to it as LSI from now on) account. Lightning Source is part of the Ingram group. This means that all your books listed in the digital library of Lightning Source are, for a special fee (used to be $50 but it is now $85), included in the Advanced Ingram Catalog (AIC)

Many people have asked me if it is worth including your book in the Advanced Catalogue and I can only say this; I have almost two hundred books in print with Ingram/LSI - of that I have paid two or three times (when I was a rookie) for the Advanced Catalogue. Now multiply this $60 by two hundred. That is how much I have saved! Those who will buy my books have. I suspect the bowkers database is just as good of the listing as the AIC.

You see, you will not just publish one book! If all goes well you will publish hundreds!

In the beginning, I have always opted-in for this feature, but later after having some discussions with other publishers, it has turned out that spending this money yielded no discernible benefit. Now, I save this $60 every time I publish a book. This saving means, newly found funds for a dinner out with my family.

By listing your titles at LSI, they will become available to the largest bookstores in the nation. When you visit Barnes and Noble next time, you can check you title's availability on their online system scattered around the store. You will find it, and anyone visiting the store can order your book.

Working with LSI is not only benefiting the publisher in terms of US sales and reach, but LSI also has a printing branch in the UK. As English language books are becoming ever more popular in the world, your next title can become known for example in Finland or in the Czech Republic as well.

Unfortunately, opening an account with LSI takes some time. Every single form must be downloaded, filled out, signed and faxed back to their headquarters.

Before you can effectively use the account now opened at LSI, you will need to be established as a publisher at Bowkers. R.R.Bowker is a non-profit organization that maintains publisher information, ISBN numbers (otherwise known as an International

Standard Book Number and a database called Books in Print.

As a new publisher you must own the ISBN numbers which you will be assigned. Recently Bowker has increased the price of their popular 10 ISBN packages to $250 but a better deal is the 100 ISBNs for $575.

After you have purchased your 100 lot of ISBNs you are to set up the title information in the Bowker database. This database is accessed by thousands of bookstores, wholesalers, libraries and other literary professionals.

R.R. Bowker, having a windfall from increasing their monopolistic prices, has decided to invest in a new website and database. Bowkerlink.com for the time being remains as is. The new database/web site is called myidentifiers.com. Both require the same password you set up with R.R. Bowker, while getting your identity as a publisher.

While myidentifiers.com is a newer web site from Bowker, the original way of keeping the book in print database updated is via bowkerlink.com.

There is a nominal charge for setting up a title in digital format at LSI. At the writing of this book, the cost is $85. After a while this charge would be forgiven but for a few years you must pay this. I guess it is a fee for education on how to submit a flawless pdf. I must warn you that title setup is not a trivial task. The cover and book PDF must be in strict adherence to the specifications supplied by LSI. Before you upload anything, you must read the specifications and guidelines. The LSI website supplies templates for book covers in the form of an online cover template generator. It factors into it the page count, the bleed margins and all pertinent information, like the size and dimensions of your book.

My Rules for Using Lightning Sourceource (LSI).

If you wish to publish public domain books in unaltered format, of which Amazon already has several editions listed, I do not recommend using LSI. There is absolutely no guarantee that Amazon will pick up your book. The exception to this is if you use a public domain book as basis for your book and you annotate or otherwise add content and material of your own rendering it a new publication. Of course, many people hate Amazon and would rather buy from other online book sellers, but the volume will be minuscule.

Following this rule will benefit you in multiple ways. You will be saving the setup charge of LSI for a book that will likely not sell that many copies. The other benefits will be outlined further in this chapter.

My Rule in listing public domain paperback books, I sometimes use Amazon KDP for public domain books that I am not the exclusive supplier of, and that I have not researched the copyright status of. Removing a title from Amazon KDP will cost far less than closing a title in LSI if there are any unforeseen legal challenges. However, Amazon can close your KDP account if such violations occur regularly.

You see, if the book is not wordy of hardcover it can be frustrating to see all the publishers who are not on Ingram cutting costs to the bare minimum.

LSI/Ingram have made changes to their website to offer more user friendly features. After you have submitted your title to LSI, you must wait for your POD client service representative to verify if it complies with their internal standards. If for some reason there is something to fix or questionable about the cover or the book, it will be communicated to you via e-mail. However now there is an initial software check to weed out most of the issues.

Make sure that you have read and understand the standards and requirements mandated by LSI for digital file submission or any resubmission and verifications will cost you additional money, even if you do the change. This is because LSI charges you for any extra time they need to spend on your title. It is assumed that either you are an expert in setting up a digital book for their database/catalog or it is within your means to hire someone.

The number of popular, well received books you submit to LSI will determine your success as a publisher. It is of the utmost importance that you do not waste costly ISBN numbers and pricey setup cost to poorly selling titles.

LSI charges some publishers $12 per title for each full calendar year as a listing fee. Depending on your relationship and quantity of books listed this fee maybe reduced under a new policy. This might sound trivial but if you have ten titles that do not sell at all, this in turn, translates into a $120 yearly cost for your publishing business.

LSI will remove titles that do not sell at your request. Be sure that poor sales cannot be somehow remedied, because resubmitting the book will also cost you, if you for some reason later change your mind.

For this and some other reasons, explained later in this book, I have started working with Amazon KDP (fully explained in chapter IX) is not meant to replace LSI in your publishing business, but rather strategically complement it.

Discount percentage with LSI

Amazon requires a whopping 55-percent discount when and if you do business directly through them. This creates a false illusion to many publishers that the Lightning Source discount should be

55-percent as well. This is a huge mistake. You are giving up way too much with this. If your books are a rendition on an existing Public Domain theme with fresh content, illustration, and generous editorials I used to set the discount at 35-percent. If your book is an original, how- to book, some publishers claim as low as a 40-percent discount.[4] Use your common sense.

Even if you are republishing something out of print, a 55-percent discount is giving away the store. Why?

Traditionally discounts were created for wholesale purchases buying in volume. Not printing one off, for a sale off some web-page. If you are afraid that Amazon will not pick up your public domain book you can experiment. Start off at 55-percent and once Amazon starts selling it you can change the discount percentage. Is this immoral or illegal switch and bait? I do not think so. You are free to change the discount and they are free not ordering via LSI. Be careful here and use good judgment, do not get too greedy. It pays to create unique content.

Other online booksellers.

Amazon is a huge company and they are playing games with small businesses thus there is a backlash against them. Smaller online booksellers honed on the fact that Amazon is no longer in a book business, despite the fact that it still sells books. If you are partner with Ingram, either as LSI or Ingram/Spark, these book-sellers[5] will pick up your books. Fortunately, lot of people prefer to buy from a small, independent business. Sadly, in the spring of 2023, Amazon closed down BookDepository[6], a huge book seller in the UK that used to have free shipping. This cost me a lot of royalty revenue.

In summary, I recommend using LSI only without the restrictions of KDP. Amazon can and does close accounts arbitrarily. There are legal teams specializing for this exclusively.

---

4   The new discount is 40-percent for the US and 30-percent worldwide.

5   Alibris, Books-a-Million, Powel's Books are the bigger ones in the US. In the UK and Europe are a many more.

6   Founded in the United Kingdom in 2004, Book Depository sells over 20 million books, and offers free delivery — with no minimum spend — to more than 120 countries, according to its website.

VIII. How to Market Your Business

Marketing is essential in all businesses. In this book the reader will be guided to the most cost effective methods. Internet marketing is not new but it changes daily. This chapter addresses both Internet and brick and mortar marketing. It is suggested to have several web sites for your publishing business. The main website is the publisher's website. Here you should tell about your genre or theme, you should have a catalog, a blog if you are so inclined and even a searchable book database. This chapter is mainly for those who are creative and value add a public domain works or perhaps write their own cookbook. So in individual website should be for any new, derivative work that is perhaps based on a public domain but heavily annotated and perhaps illustrated The criterion of this is that the book must be fresh and unique enough to dedicate an individual website for it. For example: building, designing and maintaining a website is overkill if you decided to republish Plato's Republic.

Web design

I was fortunate having spent two decades in IT and web programming working for Fortune 500 companies. I have learned doing HTML and web-layout, with JavaScript's and Java while companies paid me a very good hourly rate for my efforts. Yet, I have paid freelance people for web design and simple graphics work.

Why? It was because it is labor intensive and takes some good creative ideas that I momentarily lacked. After the dot com crash, the hourly rate for IT guys had dropped drastically. I still consider my time valuable enough to have justified the occasional hire of a freelancer. Further, hiring a freelancer on the cheap allows your business to leverage and reinvest your book sales profits into your own business.

A one-man company can only do so much.

According to Morris Rosenthal, the expert on web based, on-demand publishing and book marketing, a book based web page needs to be different than any other commercial web page. This is how he puts it on his web page FonerBooks.com.

"Most important of all, don't pay a website designer thousands of dollars to build you a website. You wouldn't pay $30 for a gallon of milk, so don't pay a website designer ten times what they're worth.

Word press is a free, open source platform to build a website and have a Book Listing database added on as one of the many Word press plugins.

Building an author platform isn't about technology or aesthetics, it's about content, and the only person who can create that content is you." So do what I do. Pay for simple graphics work and some basic layout design (unless you are inspired to get into that art) and use some online freelance services such as RentaCoder.com. Focus on the content!

Rentacoder was purchased by UpWorks.com and the bidding feature was sadly removed.

Still. I have personally tried eLance and UpWorks.com and favor UpWork.com, for their prices, service and reliability. Their business model is not that unique, you post a job on their web site, and then after finding a matching candidate, you place the bid amount in escrow with the service provider. They hold the funds until completion and mitigate any conflicts or issues arising. The escrow concept is what makes these job sites valuable. Unless you are 100-percent satisfied with the work, the service provider will not get paid. If you use a freelance web site long enough (like me) eventually you will run into someone who will take you for a fool. In web design there are several providers of free and low cost templates. Be careful that the provider is not overcharging you for a free template he just downloaded. It is common practice. I always post a requirement for original work. UpWorks.com has fine selection criteria for geographical locations and proficiency of the English language. Using software talent from India used to be a fad. Twenty years ago they were reliable and cheap. Nowadays they are often as expensive as their counterparts elsewhere.

I have a great deal of admiration for Indian software talent. I have worked with them for years and I know what some of them are capable of. However, not all Indian software is superb, as not all Japanese cars are above requiring repairs.

Indians and Pakistanis are not easy to deal with as business people. They can outsmart the best and often they make a sport of doing just that.

Use common sense. If the provider is giving you what looks like a template, alert UpWorks' dispute resolution service. I must say this: problems like this are not common place. Be generous and kind. If you are impossible to please, using cheap freelancers will not work for you. Do not quibble over minor things. Release the funds if the other party has done his part.

Google AdWords

Certain books are considered to be a niche market, and for that they can command higher prices. These are trading/finance books and scientific/medical titles. For these books and for these books alone you could use Google Adwords.

Google Adwords would fill a chapter by itself. It suffices to say that you can advertise your business by selecting other web sites in the same genre as your book or website.

Keep in mind that Google AdWords, as the name implies, is based on keywords. Choose a unique keyword and the cost will be less, if you choose a popular keyword obviously the cost will be commensurate.

As for an average public domain book selling for $9.95-$12.95 on Amazon I would not recommend this marketing venue as the cost will far outweigh the benefits.

Making retail sales versus selling wholesale is a complex and emotional issue.

Obviously the emphasis on my way of publishing is that as with any business, it is well worth the effort to sell only wholesale and avoid direct dealing with the customer. Retail selling has the added drawback of collecting sales tax and the need to have a merchant account for credit card processing and the dreaded shipping. I have had a merchant account before and I used to ship my Course for Traders, and believe me it is tedious and unrewarding. Never again, will I do this!

Make your own Catalog The cheapest way to put the word out about your new publishing business is to create a book catalog that is available online and selectively in print. The catalog can be a word document and uploaded to your website as a PDF file.

To create a PDF file, I now use Adobe InDesign CC 2019 (Adobe has moved to a subscription model).

I have sent my catalog to independent bookstores several times by hand.

Quora and other social media.

Quora is a new web site and interestingly the founders of Quora were executives at Facebook. The site is a question answer format for all experts and no-real-experts alike.

Quora users answer to any or all pertinent questions while readers rate their answers. Many authors would use their book excerpts while listing the book, on Amazon. After the lens is completed (it is a rather easy and user friendly site), Enough talk about this, go ahead and try it. As a recent move Quora answers can be promoted, for a fee, of course. I have never tried that so buyer beware. Facebook is filled with authors and booksellers and their advertising scheme much more straightforward and transparent than Google's.

Amazon is now accepting advertising for books and I highly recommend to budget and consider such a service. This service is only available for Amazon Sellers. We must distinguish between a publisher and an Amazon Seller. As a publisher Amazon will likely pick up and stock your books, but that is not guaranteed. Some books that they have multiple sellers will not stock, or list them as 'available in 1 or 2 month'! With print on demand the book should be available in 1 or 2 days as most cases, lists. As an Amazon seller you can list such books yourself. The caveat, you must fulfill the books or Amazon will. All listing and being Amazon seller incurs fees of course.

Brick and Mortar Advertising I have seen books advertised in magazines. I do not recommend paying the ad rate for a magazine unless you can arrange some sort of a barter system, which is amazingly commonplace in the new economy of the 21st century.

Bartering for magazine ads can be done by you offering to write a feature article on a subject that of course you must be knowledgeable with. After the article is written, submitted and approved by the editor, in the next issue you will be given an ad space previously agreed upon. It is a win-win situation; the Magazine gains an article for free and the book publisher (that is you) gets to advertise something for free.

You are wondering if this is possible, or I am just making this up. I know it is possible because I have done it! I am a published author in the financial circles, even though nobody paid me a cent for my work, I got a free ad. Do not attempt to do this with a stranger. You must first establish a relationship with the owner or the chief editor of the magazine. The magazine must be relevant in terms of theme and genre of their publication and hungry enough to approach positively this creative bartering scheme.

American Booksellers Association (ABA) Marketing Proogram Every month a box measuring 18-1/2" x 18-1/2" x 4" is sent to each of the 900 actively participating IndieBound stores, filled with galleys, ARCs, finished books, excerpt booklets, posters, sell sheets, catalogs, easelbacks, bookmarks, postcards, and sundry other items provided by American Booksellers Association ((ABA) Publisher Partners.

The Independent Book Publishers Association (IBPA) The Independent Book Publishers Association ((IBPA) can help your publishing business in marketing, book fairs and with other invaluable resources. Their membership is cheaper than ABA's.

IBPA can help in the form of direct mail, as a marketing co-op.

They can facilitate lower cost promotional mailings to book buyers, reviewers and other organizations who might be interested in your book.

The word publishing was not registered as long domain names are not advantageous. In my opinion and experience you also would want to limit all your domain names as .com, as it is the universal and international domain name appendage. It is the most prestigious, least limiting by country or theme. Others are .biz, .gov (reserved for government entities) and so on. Since an English language publishing company or even a book is meant to be international in its scope, I am very happy that I could reserve the domain name above.

Note: I would avoid dashes and other characters as much as possible from domain name selection, but it is of lesser importance than a good short name, that people easily remember and identify with. I could write more on this subject as internet basics but there are several good books out there already and much of this information is available online for free. Use your favorite search engine and study this subject in depth. The scope of this book is only to keep you alert and aware of this, not to expand on the subject in detail.

The Indie bound Movement If you consider all the marketing schemes and the way we are being directed to consumerism today, you can't be surprised that big companies offering big discounts on large amounts of stuff are doing extremely well. Now, though, we really need to take a moment to consider these deals we take advantage of and find out what we are really doing.

First, we are contributing to global warming by purchasing goods from all over the country and frequently overseas, second we are purchasing goods at a discount but the discount is coming from employee benefits, third we are all getting generic mass produced goods and overlooking the benefit of different real craftsmanship available from our local producers.

When you hear about global warming, you hear a number of different opinions on the subject. Lately, there is much discussion over leaving a carbon footprint. Since the industrial revolution humans have been impacting the environment with excess additional carbon emissions, which in turn is changing the air and plant life around us. We don't know exactly what will happen over time; all the forecasts paint a very grim picture.

With the purchase of goods and basic materials that have been shipped world-wide we contribute to the carbon imprint. Different modes of transportation add to the environmental impact. Buying local goods reduces the amount of traffic needed to get goods and materials to consumers. Between planes, trains and automobiles, with goods from overseas you are increasing the number of carbon emissions by at least 1200 times over buying things from local producers.

If you go into a store with many items and purchase at a deep discount then you are probably congratulating yourself on getting such a deal. What you might not know is where the saving is coming from; it certainly isn't on transportation costs. The decrease in price is coming from people's salaries directly, or the benefits they are entitled to.

The large store you frequent might employ people in the community, but their benefits and wages are not necessarily comparable to other companies that produce the same types of goods. It has been studied and found that if you "spend $100 at a locally owned store and $68 of that stays in your community. Spend the same $100 at a national chain, and your community only sees $43," which is an unfortunate and low statistic. This also means that people who work at large organizations have less money to re-invest directly in their community.

As well as under-compensating employees, buying mass produced goods overlooks the beauty and quality available in locally made items. Local artists might not get enough exposure to sell the majority of items they produce, and they are also limited to the audience for the items they sell. Even people who produce goods of a different nature may not have the funds available to market and ship items world-wide. Really, with a market within the local community they should not be expected to reduce their already slim profit margin in an effort to ship overseas when there are people within easily reachable distances that are perfectly capable of purchasing their goods.

What the independent movement in the United State tries to do, and is doing, is raise awareness of the issues that arise when people start putting their business into large corporations and neglecting the smaller ones. It also tries to give small businesses opportunities to do more business, and provides information portals for individuals who want to support the independent movement but are just not sure how.

The internet is a tool that the independent movement is using in order to raise awareness of local United States businesses. While the internet is also at fault for generating a means by which much of the international trading is done, it is a very useful information portal.

New websites are being developed by independent movement groups that give local businesses and crafts people the ability to market their wares online. If you were to research the sites you would note that they include references to places you can go where members of the independent movement go for information. These places include details on bookstores, publishers, websites and details of music associations committed to independent media.

Independent bookstores have a number of books available for those interested in learning about the independent movement. The independent bookstores also network together and report book lists back on what the indie members are purchasing and reading most. You can find a great number of bookstores; some examples include News beat and East West books in Sacramento, CA which open their doors to people who want to know the truth.

In order to get the truthful and sometimes radical information out about the independent movement a number of publishers have set up shop. They generally include all volunteer staff that is committed to providing truthful accounts of information and sources. Most states have an independent media organization, and the website indemedia.us provides a great deal of independent media communications data.

Other publishers, like the Houston Independent Media Center, the Portland Independent Media Center and the Independent Media in Austin, TX provide different available portals for individuals in the community that create goods or works that require exposure. In Austin, TX there is an event called STAPLE! The Independent Media Expo that is held yearly and has individuals to encourage communication between audiences and the individuals who produce goods.

Independent media websites are also available and allow people world-wide to share stories and accounts of activities that are generally not found in the daily newspapers. One such website (http://www.indymedia.org/en/) is currently running information on government changes (outside the US) which will impact us in different ways, accounts of torture and murders outside our immediate neighborhoods, and court decisions. All these articles are available because of the independent media movement's progress with regards to free speech.

Music products that are produced without funding from major record labels are indie record labels. In the US independent record labels are produced by the A2IM or American Association of Independent Music, in the UK by the Association of Independent Music and in Australia by the Australian Independent Records Labels Association.

The focus of independent music associations is to ensure that independent musicians receive the same type of advantages of those who have signed with major record labels, including access to mainstream media types (radio and television), promoting legislation favoring independent labels, and demonstrating the cultural and economic importance of independent labels.

In order for small local businesses to be successful they rely on advertisement of their business. Sometimes it is possible that a lot of advertising is done through word of mouth alone, but it is rare. With the cost of advertising high, and start up businesses not having a lot of funding available to utilize some modes of advertising, starting and keeping a local business going is very difficult.

Many Independent media groups (such as the Center for Independent Media) are focused as well on the education of local writers and business owners in order to show them ways of using new technologies to enhance their prospects. This is also in the best interests of creating diversity in media and journalism, since the independent media movement relies on finding true accounts of stories written by regular citizens.

Websites are now open that cater to the individuals who wish to promote independent products. They allow a place for business owners to advertise freely and also declare themselves as independent organizations that believe in the independent media movement.

Promoting awareness of the independent media movement is a challenge in itself. With the majority of money making going on with high-profile companies, independent retailers often have difficulty finding people already in public positions to listen and advocate their services. People who do volunteer to publicly advertise the availability of independent media services are often downplayed as radicals or "conspiracy theorists".

Even though free speech is the rule in most of the Western world, governments do not actively pursue courses which would enable the public to learn of activities that might not be seen as purely wholesome, so directing the masses to websites that publish truthful articles and accounts of their personal activities isn't a priority from a governmental point of view.

In fact, because of the money and controversy that can arise from different facets of the independent media movement, there are many people and companies that try to suppress the information available and product availability because it is not in their best interests. There have been attempts by different organizations to standardize how and when freedoms of rights and expression should be communicated, but they are largely unsuccessful because of the diversity of opinion of freedom of rights and expression.

In light of this it seems unlikely that there is an independent media movement at all. The organizations that are in existence frequently communicate to ensure that they know that the other exists, and they provide linkages in order for people from different communities to specialize in what they need. This helps if someone is looking for local goods but can only find them local to another community.

One of the biggest commitments independent media has committed to is educating the public. This includes providing people who are willing to volunteer their time and bring awareness in different locations. Independently run bookstores are a great source of educating people about the independent media movement. People also need to be tech savvy enough to take advantage of the opportunities available for activities in the independent media movement.

Holding craft or fair events where local businesses are registered is also one way that the independent media movement is advertised. The conglomeration of websites available gives access to independent media companies which would not have been available prior to the Internet.

For the individual who is not quite sure how to start an involvement in the independent media movement it would be best to consult an Independent Media group directly. If the individual has skills that can be applied, and is willing to volunteer, independent media groups are happy to have anyone willing to offer their services.

When you first hear of the independent media movement you might go in expecting it to be just one small company, but because of their inter-joined nature there are a number of possible things you can do to start off in support of independent media businesses. You will also be surprised that a quick search can yield you a larger variety of services than you thought possible.

It is important in countries that promote themselves as free speech countries that independent media companies exist and are given an opportunity to flourish. It is unfortunate that when searching out information on the Independent Media Movement, you come across many stories that aren't successful. If you were to do a search you would come across many websites that advertise started on such-and-such a date and ended less than a year later.

It requires a true commitment to the independent media way to start and maintain an independent business, whether it is in the book trade, publishing, journals or producing local works of art. Even with the most dedicated individual, you also need to have the survivor instincts to find the resources out there to promote your business.

For those people who have made it their lifelong commitment to freedom of speech and freedom of business the payoff is seldom in monetary. The type of person who would be able to do well at this industry would have to be one not motivated by money, but motivated by the good of the community, and would have to be satisfied with that as their reward.

As time goes on governments may be more concerned with the welfare of the environment than the welfare of the salaries of government officials and begin promoting local businesses directly. In the meanwhile the Internet proves to be their main mode of advertisement to those not already involved.

IX. Search Engine Optimization (SEO)

This is not for the faint hearted and computer illiterate, but as scary as this subject may sound, it is very simple. My advice to the not-so-computer savvy is to hire someone to optimize your web pages for search engines.

What is Search Engine Optimization Search Engine Optimization is the process of improving the volume and/or quality of traffic to a web site by considering how search engines work and how people look for results.

Both parts of this must be considered when planning your SEO strategy; one without the other will garner great results for low-competitor search terms, or will return poor results for competitive search terms.

For example, if your web site promoted a book written on the benefits of healthy eating, you may wish to be ranked for the term "healthy eating". This term is a very competitive one, with many thousands of companies all vying to have the best results for it.

However, if you were to optimize your site for the term "healthy eating will make me fitter", you would find that it was much easier to rank for this term – as there are fewer competitors wanting to be optimized for the term – but no person uses this as a search term.

In essence, you have created a strategy that will give you results that no one is looking for. This is why you must have both facets of the process covered when considering your own SEO strategy.

How Do Search Engines Rank There are many different search engines, all using different techniques to determine how important your page is for a particular term, phrase or subject. The largest search engine is Google – and it uses a constantly evolving, dynamic algorithm to calculate the various positions for individual web pages. This algorithm is also secret. Why Secret? Well, to put it plainly, if it were publicly available, it would be easier for search engine experts to tailor content, site structure and more in order to influence the ranking. Instead, Google tries to use the natural democratic nature of the Internet in order to drive its results.

Google PageRank™

Google uses the algorithm to rank pages on a scale between 0 and 10. Although the scale has almost infinite ranking positions, for ease of use it only displays whole integers in the PageRank toolbar.

Each indexed web page is assigned an individual ranking, or level of importance, by Google based on a number of factors.

Back Links

Each time a site links to you, Google takes this as a "vote" for your site. The more links, the more votes, the better the rank. It's not just the number of votes though. If the PageRank of the site linking to yours is higher, then its vote is worth more. So, a single link from a PR5 site is worth more than 4 links from PR1 sites.

Outbound Links There is a cloud to go with the silver lining. A page can only have one Page Rank score. And every outbound link from that page (including internal links) takes a share of that ranking.

So, if you have a link from a PR5 page, but that page has 99 other links, then you are only receiving 1/100th of the PR5. In this instance, a link from a PR1 page is actually better than the PR5 page link.

Outbound Link Quality You have no control over which sites link to you. For this reason, if you are linked to by an unsavory site (a link farm, banned content, pornography etc), your site is not penalized by Google.

However, you can control the quality of sites that you link to. For this reason, if you have an outbound link to an unsavory site, you will be penalized and, in extreme cases, removed from Google's index completely.

Anchor Text Each link to your web page requires an anchor. This can be an image or text that forms the hyperlink. Google, and other search engines, look at the text used or, in the case of images, the alt text to determine the nature of the link. This helps Google to determine what content your site is optimized for and is one of the most underused techniques in SEO. Don't believe me? Let us do a little experiment, shall we? Try a search for "Click Here" in Google. What's the number one result? The top page search result is "Adobe - Adobe Reader". Now open the page for Adobe (http://get. adobe.com/uk/reader/). Can you see the term "click here" anywhere on the page? No. It's not there. Yet it ranks #1 for the search term. This is because many thousands of web pages have a link to the Adobe site with the anchor text "click here" in order to download the latest version of their Adobe Reader software. Remember this with your off-the-pageSEO strategy (covered later in this chapter) These techniques are predominantly off-the-page activities and will give the biggest SEO benefits. However, there are also many things that can be done on the-page, which many people looking to improve their rankings miss.

Off-TheThe-Page and OnPage and On-TheThe-Page SEO There

are two methods of SEO that can be done – and they are not exclusive; you can – and should – do both. On-the-page SEO covers all of the activities that you can do on your website. Off-the-page SEO covers all activities that are completed away from your website on other web pages/sites. We've already covered some of the off-the-page activities. The other main activities that you should do away from your site are:

Directory Submissions Submit your website to all major directories. DMOZ is the main, free index and should be considered for any one that is serious about driving traffic. Of course your site should also be submitted to and indexed by Google, Yahoo!, Ask and Bing (formerly MSN Search and Live Search).

Article Submission If your site has any amount of content (and it should), you should consider writing articles, press releases and other documents for posting to article directories and news outlets.

The articles should be keyword-rich (see on-the-page) and include a link back to your site with suitable anchor text. These can be submitted to article sites such as ezinearticles.com, article-hut. com and even digg.com. You could even upload to Facebook, Bebo and other social networking sites too.

On-the-page activities are much easier for you to control; not least of all because they all take place within your own site. As these are all within your control, they do not give as much benefit to your ranking as off-the-page SEO. However, many webmasters do not consider all on-the-page examples here, and they are missing out on some easy benefits.

Meta Tags

Each web page has several Meta tags available. "Description", "Keywords", "Author", "last updated" – the list is immense. Over the course of time, many of these tags have been abused by web developers and now are given varying levels of notice by the search engines. Some are ignored completely. It is important to complete the following Meta tags for your site:

Metaname="description"content="yourcontenthere" This tag provides the description that appears on your search engine result in Google. Although it has no (known) weight with ranking, it is presented to end users and should be interesting enough to make them click through to your site. It should be different for every page.

Metaname="tile"content="yourcontentherre" Although not technically a Meta tag, the titeelementis the single most important piece of information in the head section of your HTML. The title helps Google et al to identify what your page is all about. It should be short and to the point, as the more words you have, the less their individual impact will be. For example, if your title is three words long and contains the word "healthy", this will be regarded as the 3rdmost important search term in your page. If your page title is "healthy eating can make you thin", the word "can" is just as important as the word "healthy", insofar as keyword density is concerned. Google seems to offer slightly more weight for words earlier in the sentence. Each page title should be unique and relevant to your page. Duplicate titles across pages can be penalized by Google.

Metaname="keywords"content="your,content,here" The keywords Meta tag has been abused over the years and no longer has any importance to Google. However, some other search engines, such as Yahoo!, do still use the keywords tag and it should be added to all of your pages.

The other Meta tags are primarily used to provide information to web developers rather than to search engines. Some bespoke search engines will use tags such as "author" and "version". However, these are out of scope for this article.

HTML Structure Search engines love valid coding. The simpler your coding is, the easier it is for the search engines to "crawl" your site content. And the easier it is to "crawl", the easier it is to index your pages into the search engines.

Also, web crawlers look at your page from the top down. So any additional coding in the header area (such as superfluous Meta tags and JavaScript) actually reduces the crawler's ability to index your page content.

Adding your JavaScript calls to the bottom of your page (where possible) will not only speed up your page load time for the user, it also improves the crawler's efficiency too.

CSS Structure Cascading Style Sheets allow for your site content to be kept completely separate from your site styling. As crawlers only look at your HTML – the content – having a valid CSSdriven site is beneficial to your SEO strategy.

Internal Anchor Text

This is the most missed on-the-page strategy of all web developers. Just as with external back links, each internal link has an image or text that forms your anchor. These can be optimized on your internal pages too. For example, if you have a contact us page, you can link to it with "click here". This will optimize the contact us page for the term "click here". This is clearly a poor idea. Optimizing the anchor text to something such as "Contact Company name" is much better.

Content and Keywords The most important thing about your web page is the content shown on it. Google knows it; your customers know it; you know it. If your content contains the search phrases you wish to optimize for, it stands a far better chance of being ranked for those terms. Combined with the title element, this gives the biggest single benefit to your on-the-page program. There are many other on-the-page activities that can be completed. Alt tags for images, clearing empty whitespace from your coding and positioning of key phrases within your content can all help to improve your ranking.

Word of Advice

Make sure that you do not fall for the unscrupulous pitch of a "snake oil" salesman who might offer to use methods such as farms and keyword stuffing that degrade both the relevance of search results and the user experience of search engines. Search engines do look for sites that employ these techniques in order to remove them from their indices. I am sure you have visited websites that have a web page called site map. There is a good reason for this and it burgeoned into the latest Google supported SEO technology.

The Site-maps protocol allows you to inform search engines about URLs (or addresses of individual sub-pages) on a website that is available for crawling. A Sitemap is an XML file that lists the URLs for a site. It allows you to include additional information about each URL: when it was last updated, how often it changes, and how important it is in relation to other pages in the site. This allows search engines to "crawl" the site more intelligently. Site maps are a URL inclusion protocol and complement robots.txt, which is an URL exclusion protocol. The Site maps protocol also allows the Site map to be a simple list of URLs in a text file. The file specifications of XML Site maps apply to text Site maps as well; the file must be UTF-8 encoded, and cannot be more than 10MB large or contain more than 50,000 URLs, but can be compressed as a gzip file. If Sitemaps are submitted directly to a search engine (pinged), it will return status information and any processing errors. The details involved with submission will vary with the different search engines. The location of the Site map can also be included in the robots.txt file by adding the following line to robots.txt:

Site map: <sitemap_location>

I am not a SEO expert, yet I have managed with my web site somehow. My adventure has involved lots of online research and certain basic knowledge on computing and the Internet ins and outs. Here are some questions and suggestions when looking for a SEO consultant.

How Do You Pick a Great SEO Expert?

Do a Google search for "SEO Expert". How many results do you see? I receive over 13-million results. The SEO market is saturated with companies and individuals claiming that they can get you great rankings and drive traffic to your website. With so many experts available, whom should you choose? The purpose of this chapter is to help to guide your choice with some simple questions that you should be asking of any potential Search Engine Optimization expert before you let them loose on your campaign.

Question#1:

Can you get me to the top of the search engine results pages (SERPs)?

The answer you want is "no".

No one, even Google themselves, can guarantee your position through organic search results. Organic results are from normal, natural searches by users, not influenced by any outside factor such as payment for listing. You can guarantee first three positions on Google if you are prepared to pay for a sponsored link. But why would you pay an SEO "expert" to do this for you if you can approach Google yourself, without any SEO experience, and achieve the same result?

Bottom line: If an SEO expert promises to get you into a specific position – top of the results; top ten; first page etc. – they are either lying or do not understand the nature of search engine rankings. Either way, they're not for you.

Question#2:

Will you need to change my website?

The answer that you want is "Yes" – or at least "let's take a look at your site and make a decision". SEO can be conducted in two styles: on-the-page and of-the-page. Although off-the-page work delivers greater results because of the way search engine ranking algorithms work, many so-called "experts" completely miss the importance of optimizing your actual web pages. Your content, your site structure, the load time, outbound links, code validity, the ease with which search engine spiders "crawl" your site. All of these factors, and more, will ultimately affect the way your site will eventually be ranked. If your SEO guy doesn't want to look at your site and at least review the work that you have completed already, they don't know what they're doing. And, if they don't know what they're doing, do you really want them to be in charge of guiding customers to your site? I didn't think so.

Question#3:What software do you use for SEO? The answer you're looking for is "I use some where appropriate, but you can't beat some manual, hands-on work". There are loads of software packages available to improve your page ranking, and some work better than others. Having said that, there are some instances where old fashioned manual work is the key to great results. If your expert uses an automated system to submit your site URL to directories, acquire back links or add content to article sites, these will not give you as great a benefit as manual submissions. Likewise, if your SEO expert sends automated, template-based emails to other webmasters asking for reciprocal links, they are very likely to be less successful than sending tailored emails, individually addressing their interest in why they want to exchange links. This SEO software is available to anyone – not just SEO experts. If you are paying a long-term partner to maintain and improve your ranking using only automated solutions, then why wouldn't you simply invest in the software yourself?

Question#4:

How do you know if my SEO campaign is being successful?

The answer you are wanting is "by the conversion rate". If you receive answers such as "the amount of traffic", "the number of page views", "your PageRank" or "the position of your site in the SERPs", your expert is not a true SEO expert. A true SEO expert understands that getting people to your site is only one stage in a successful strategy. Increasing your visitors from 100 per day to 1,000,000 per day does nothing if those visitors are still not buying your products and/or services. In fact, you'll probably be in a worse position, having increased your bandwidth usage and, therefore, the cost of running your site. The whole purpose of increasing your site visibility is to get more of the right people to your web pages, and for those people to convert into sales. If this concept seems alien to your SEO expert, there are better experts out there that will deliver a successful SEO campaign.

Question#5:

Are there any practices that we shouldn't do?

The answer should be "absolutely".

I can give you some tips that will drive traffic to your site and put you at the top of the search engines within a very short period of time. You can then pay me and our business is concluded; just in time for your site to be completely removed from the search engine index. As with most things in life, there are two ways to get results. We can do it the correct way, which is more work and takes longer to see the results, or we can do it in a quick and dirty way that shows results quickly but is also spotted and punished just as quickly. SEO is no exception. There are "White Hat" and "Black Hat" SEO experts, so named because of old Western films, in which the bad guys always wore black hats whilst the heroes wore white.

White Hat SEO is hard work. But it delivers results that are long-term and strong. Black Hat SEO can be done very easily and can deliver results that a layman might interpret as a job well done. But, as we've already mentioned, this short-term gain won't last forever and depending on the actions taken, can make your website disappear completely from Google et al. Essentially, Black Hat SEO delivers higher search engine ranking results in an unethical manner.

So, what practices come with the black head wear?

Hidden Text

Search engines use your content and keyword weight to determine what your page is about and how important it is. Unfortunately, you can't just write "seo seo seo search engine seo seo google seo seo search engine google" etc all over your page, as this will look hideous to your human visitors.

Black hat SEO has a way around this. Add the text to your page, but make it the same color as your background. That way, your human visitors won't see it, but the search engine crawlers will spot it in your HTML code. Genius!

Nope. Google is very much on top of this technique. Even having text that is a similar color to your background can land you in hot water. Light grey on a white background? Say "goodbye" to your listings.

Keyword Spamming

Key word density is the ratio of how often a particular word or phrase appears within a block of content. If a web site is written for human visitors (as it should be), you would expect the keyword density to be within an acceptable tolerance.

Google knows this. If your density is too low, your site will not be ranked well for the term. If it's too high, Google's algorithm assumes that you are keyword spamming, and reduces your ranking. It can also remove you from the index.

Doorway Pages

A doorway page is a page built purely for search engines, optimized for a few short keywords/phrases, which your human visitors will never see.

Often, they are coded to show particular content for a search engine spider and different content for a human reader. On other occasions, the page uses a redirect for non-human visitors. They can also be "orphan pages"; a page that has back links to your site pages, such as your home page, but no links to itself. This means that the only way to reach it is to type in the full URL address in to your browser. Any time that you show different content to search engines compared to human visitors, it's generally a bad idea that's punished or ignored by the search engines.

Summary If your expert can answer these 5 questions to your satisfaction, you're well on your way to a great partnership; one that can deliver tangible, stable results for your web site.

The keyword there is "partnership". SEO is a two-way street, with slow traffic and lots of road work. You will not see results in a few days – they could take as much 3-months before you start to see real benefits. And even then, these results will change as your competitors adjust their own strategies for those precious keywords.

When this happens, you need to know that the person you rely on for your SEO work isn't some fly-by-night black hat cowboy. You need the lone ranger.

X. How to Work with Amazon

Amazon started out as a humble technology company in Seattle, Washington. Amazon's founder Jeff Bezos had some revolutionary ideas on selling books on the internet and offering small publishers and authors a viable venue on name recognition and marketing their books.

The whole secret of Amazon's book selling is pairing up books with other contents that are similar, and the customer reviews that can be a hotbed of heated arguments and controversial criticism. Exactly the kind of attention a publisher or author would want!

First, we must learn what books sell well on Amazon and the reasons for success or failure. This can easily be accomplished by doing an Amazon search for the subject or subjects you are considering publishing on Amazon. At the end of the search, Amazon will provide a list of candidates that match your search criteria. You can see those books; study them by reading the editorials and reviews, good or bad. Make sure you check out Amazon's sales rank, to gauge the possibility of success or failure for your book.

If you are considering republishing a title that shows up with a half dozen other publishers and the sales rank is poor, then you can be assured that you will not sell too many of that title.

When you choose to rework public domain information to the extent of having a need to give a new title, a wise and careful selection of the title and subtitle can affect your book sales on Amazon. The reason for this is Amazon's online presence and the fact that Internet Search engines "crawl" and index Amazon book pages too. Book titles sometimes seem too lengthy and verbose at first, only to reveal the smart Search Engine Optimization techniques and careful planning in selecting the titles and subtitles.

For example, did the author of " Top Self Publishing Firms: How Writers Get Published, Sell More Books, And Rise To The Top: And Make Money Working From Home With The Best Print On Demand Self-Publishing Companies" has named his book this long-winded by accident? I do not think so.

Get Commented on Amazon

Once your book is listed on Amazon, your goal is to get as many favorable comments as possible. This means you must be active on Amazon. You should open an account as a buyer. In addition you can open an account as a publisher and if you have literary ambitions, as an author as well. Navigating on Amazon can be a challenge as it is a huge site getting millions of hits.

The time to put the word out about your book is in its final phases of typesetting and formatting the book block as well as the book cover. Send them to as many willing readers who may share your interest (genre) or somehow work out a deal between authors and publishers to review each other's books.

Once you have an active account on Amazon, you can edit your existing profile there. It is your window to the millions of book buyers out there to tell them about you. Use this opportunity well.

Keep informed Amazon is a dynamic company that changes rapidly with the ever-changing business of desktop publishing and technologies. To keep abreast of the changes, you can check out Amazon's PR page.

Your books, once sold on Amazon, will each have a unique rank, called sales rank. With over three dozen titles in print, it is hard to keep up with the changes in each and every book in my catalog, but newly published books I always follow closely.

Aaron Shepard, the author of the wonderful book Aiming at Amazon, has developed a web service called Sales Rank Express to follow Amazon sales ranks with greater ease.

His website used to be www.salesrankexpress.com, but it no longer works; Amazon managed to break it too.

Being a small reprint publisher is a high-wire act between Amazon and Ingram/LSI. Amazon is a powerhouse, but Ingram is a worldwide distributor. If you find your book to be "shunned" by Amazon, you can always become an Amazon seller and provide the book from LSI by stocking the title yourself. Just make sure you are not a "professional seller," because that is around $40 per month. You must avoid this charge because the shipping cost of stocking your book, which Amazon should cover, is an expense. Of course, if you have ideas to sell other products on Amazon, being a business seller may make sense. To my knowledge, when you search the Internet for information on becoming an Amazon seller, the "professional seller" pops up, and customer service can downgrade you to "individual, whereby the monthly charge no longer applies.

If you're thinking of becoming an Amazon seller for those reprint books that are "shunned," you'd have to consider LSI/Ingram's "Bolt" program to take advantage of their volume pricing for short-run books that you'd ship to Amazon.

Other considerations include shipping costs and turnaround time.

As an Amazon seller, when it is time to restock your Amazon warehouse bin, it is up to you. You only get paid when the books sell, but you will enjoy a very low shipping rate. If you can find an offset printer that uses the Amazon shipping label (by logging into your Seller account), you will enjoy both cheap shipping and a possibly lower cost of printing.

Recent developments put LSI ahead of Amazon KDP. LSI approves a book automatically without waiting for the 72+ hours that Amazon takes.

XI. How to Work with Amazon KDP

Amazon KDP(print) formerly known as CreateSpace.com a company that facilitated on demand DVD sales on the Internet. Now Amazon orphaned CreateSpace and force all print books to Amazon KDP, print.

It was their relationship with Amazon.com that got them involved in the on demand book printing business. Why Amazon orphaned them is a mystery. Some titles are still showing up as Amazon KDP Publications but there was a quality concern with that status among other things that might have initiated this rift.

Listing a book on Amazon KDP (or CS) will guarantee the publisher Amazon listing and cost effective printing charges.

As I have mentioned in Chapter V, I do not list a book with Amazon KDP that I have exclusive rights to, or a public domain book that I have the only in print publication.

The reason for this is easy to see; CS facilitates Amazon sales only. With LSI listing I have Amazon listing (via Amazon POD) but I also sell in Borders.com, Barnes and Noble online and myriads of other online booksellers that work with Ingram group also as their distributors.

Amazon KDP distribution

Amazon KDP has two choices of distribution; worldwide[7] and their own web sites at Amazon. I will use Amazon KDP in all circumstances where my book is not exclusive but with pricing or other factors that might give me a competitive edge.

Since the first publishing of this book CreateSpace had made arrangement with none other, but its arch-competitor LSI to offer CreateSpace listed book for "extended distribution". Since the discount demanded by Amazon KDP is not very friendly to the publisher, offering books as "extended" distribution is not possible unless you price the initial retail price too high.

If Amazon KDP sales prove to be flourishing and for months I hear no objections to my new publications, I then consider moving the title to LSI and removing it from KDP. Now, these techniques I have used while I had a per book setup charge. I no longer have such a concern, so I publish mainly on LSI, especially is it is a hardcover.

The reader still my find the above tactic useful as Ingram Spark

7   Same as extended distribution

- the other Ingram print on demand company charges a lesser setup fee per book ($49).

KDP has a very active and versatile forum to help new members and answer any questions that may arise from setting up a new book or DVD. There are however problems with KDP, when merged they flagged my Createspace books as copyrighted thus making me guilty of copyright violation by not clearly stating the status of the book.

Using this business paradigm there could be circumstances where you need to remove a title from Amazon KDP after you decide to go with Lightning Source distribution.

Kessinger publishing to my knowledge the largest print on demand publisher with 190,175 titles, only uses LightningSource..

XII. How to Get Publicity

There is a distinction of promoting your books individually or promoting your publishing company. Depending on the mix of your publishing repertoire the appropriate budget should be established for both venues, without ignoring either.

For example if your books are exclusively public domain books that are reprinted, promoting your company would be better served. Does this mean that you would ignore the individual titles in your catalog? The individual titles should be promoted online and offline considering every available promotional vehicle that is available for free or low cost.

This means that sending such a title to the Frankfurt Book Fair might be too excessive. Further, if you have 20 such titles, which one would deserve to be included in the Frankfurt Book Fair and which ones would not make the list?

Instead of focusing on your individual titles, you should strive to carve a niche for your publishing business. Establish it as a large print press, focus on your expertise in the genre and emphasize your careful selection of titles and judicious eye for the truth and facts in your method of picking which books to publish, and which books leave your catalog.

The number one task of the publisher after his author has finished a new book is to get this book reviewed by as many professional book reviewers as possible. This of course does not apply to public domain books.

Public domain publishers can search and quote book reviews from magazines and newspapers that were published at the original time of publication of the book they decided to reprint.

Read your Industry Publications After selecting a genre for your reprint publishing company, find and read as many related magazines as possible. Offer to write articles for those magazines if such an option exists.

How to write your own news release with prweb.com PRWeb. com allows the small business person or author to write press releases on new books or virtually any subject that might be picked up by any newswire or news agency.

It is suggested that once you have your own publishing web site up and running, you let the world know about your new business venture. Subsequently every new book published could be written up and syndicated via PRWeb.

When I started using PRWeb it had a donation based cost structure, with the basic free "visibility" of PRWeb and the higher you decide to contribute, the more the article will be featured on the PRWeb Website. Now that is changed and the free basic service is gone. The "basic visibility" is now $80. The result of doing your own PR is dubious at best. Clearly the article written and the subject must be unique and compelling to be picked up by small town news papers and radio station. Having said this, when you compare what a professional PR person or publicity agent would charge you, the $80 will be small potatoes.

There are other publicity web sites available and they will even supply you with templates for news releases.

According to John Kramer, author of 1001 Ways to Market your Books there are three facets of gaining publicity;

There must be a newsworthy event regarding your company. Your book must be unique and well written with fresh content that is timely and relates to contemporary events. It is also helpful to have an author who is well known or highly promotable.

Getting and fostering media contacts. This is important. News people and media workers have the attention span of a squirrel. You must be persistently pining for their fleeing attention. Perseverance pays off in the media world.

Follow up your contacts and keep that up until the desired results manifest.

How to Prepare a Professional Media Kit

The purpose of the Media Kit is to ease the acceptance of your press release and provide additional information about you. The components of the media kit are: the press release, cover letter, author's biography, author's photograph, copies of previous articles mentioning your book.

The press release should be written with one notion in mind, to get a phone call inquiry from the media professional. If the press release is too comprehensive and it is used ad verbatim the writer of that press release has done a poor job.

On the other hand, if the press release was written well, it will lead to interviews by media people.

The Advantage of a Printed Interview

After your successful interview by the magazine editor your interview will appear in print. The advantage of printed interviews is that they last longer. They can always be referred back to and reviewed at will. In addition, printed interviews are syndicated more often and many times they tend to lead to other, follow up stories.

How to get Radio Interviews

Typically, there are several directories and databases of expert authors that radio interviewers select from. These are all paid services but, if an interview is your goal they are well worth the cost.

There are countless other promotional ideas. Some of them are rather outrageous, such as having your own radio segment or even the whole show. How far you get in the self-promotion game depends on how high you set your goals.

XIII. e-Books the New Publishing Paradigm

This is the most exciting time for writers and publishers. The true information age has embarked on many who were previously felt locked out of the publishing business.

With the advent of Kindle and now Barnes and Noble embracing the Nook, new writers and publishers have inexpensive and powerful venues to communicate and market the written word.

There is a jungle out there and I wanted add this new chapter to clear out the "fog" and some misinformation out there. On using e-book aggregators such as smashwords.com is a waste of time. If you wish to sell e-Book for the iPod, you must sign up as an iTune content provider for e-Book but the catch is the mandatory use of Apple software hence use and Intel based MacOS machine. I am about to purchase a Mac Mini for this purpose only. I figure that the cost of this investment will be recouped in a few months. I have a strong sense that his trend will slowly kill the paperback for nonfiction titles and revitalize the hardcover for black and white, non-fiction books.

E-book Information is the main product of the 21st century, mature economies. Communication, and new technological methods of disseminating information, promptly and efficiently is the topic of this essay.

A while back you had to find and agent and a traditional publisher if you had an idea and wanted to share it with the world. This was a closed and protected market of so called experts and insiders. Nowadays, this process had become more democratic and open; anyone can do it.

Anyone can start a blog or write a book. This has opened up possibilities to all but also created clutter and information overload. The possibility to write something great is there. Not everybody is going to achieve that but with quality and uniqueness, information knows no boundaries and limits. It just comes alive.

This newfound freedom and openness had caused a paradigm shift in the book publishing industry. With the advent of on-demand-publishing and the incredible growth of Amazon.com, traditional bookstores are experiencing a decline.

I remember in the nineties the superstore concept was developed and quickly Barnes and Noble and Borders had jumped on the bandwagon and started opening them en masse in Manhattan and other urban centers. Now they are closing them or refraining from opening new ones. Since I'm no stranger to the industry I could never understand the economics of a superstore, knowing the profit margins on the book and the marketing cost and operating cost of a book mega store. I have observed the people hanging out there, most of them only browsing books, reading the magazines, seldom buying anything but coffee.

Most of the regulars are students or retired people who will not spend enough to sustain these places. Traditionally, the book business was always a gamble and environmental waste. The bookstores wanted to alleviate this by demanding unlimited returns on most merchandise, mainly on books and the published wanted the choice shelves or display spots for their favorite, newly published material. This resulted the dynamics of vying for the best "real estate" in the store and if a book not sold, quick - return to the publisher, who in turn dumped these unsalable books to the secondary merchant (for pennies on the dollar) who, would try unloading them, usually unsuccessfully. Tons of books, traditionally printed end up in the "book graveyard", also known as paper recycling plant.

This is why most newly published books start with a short run, meaning, the publisher would print 2000 copies or less and see the demand before committing more money to the project. With the numerical explosion of the published works, books in print had grown exponentially resulting financial losses for many borderline projects. A traditional publisher has several failed projects and to pull through the year and remain in the black he needs one or two best sellers. Even if the best seller would materialize, the financial gain seldom gets transferred to the author, the intellectual rights holder., the main stream publisher keeps most of it to offset his risky business model.

There is a new and better way of doing things. This essay aims to show you how. Our goal is to eliminate your risk, enhance your exposure at a minimal cost and offer you the chance to be discovered using a proven self- publishing process that first uses electronic books and if demand warrants it, on-demand publishing.

There is a distinct possibility that electronic books will accelerate encroaching into the market space of paperbacks while hardcover books will stage a modest comeback. Amazon had announced that, due to the success of the Kindle, paperback sales suffered but there was a slight increase of hardcover book sales. I guess durability and product longevity is also coming back.

It must be said; that in order to achieve success and financial independence, good, polished writing and unique and timely subject material is a must. It is my suggestion that after "finishing" a book, you put it aside and let it mature for a few weeks, after which you should read it again for smoothing out spots and areas of needed polishing. It is extremely important to fight the need for urgency the desire for completion.

The electronic book market with the advent of the Amazon Kindle and the Apple iPad is revolutionized the business of book selling. New authors can write and publish their works electronically and if it is any good, judged by the marketplace, they can either self-publish it as a printed book or try to sell it to a mainstream publisher. As most publishers are on shaky fiscal ground, "being published" usually is more of an ego gratification than a financial success. The advances are just not what they used to be. Most authors take anything at the first time, in hopes that "being published" will increase their chances with their second book.

Viral Marketing

Lets talk about the formats of e-Book. The original electronic book was made for the computer and usually it was in executable format for the personal computer market. The usability of this computer application varied from vendor to vendor. Many people started private label programs where they wrote a sales pitch in a form of a short e-book and let others buy and use their content. The application allowed the author and web page or e-mail address to be custom changed. This was an attempt to make fast money on the Internet. With the proliferation of computer viruses people have stopped opening these viral e-Book in fear that they will literarily catch a computer virus.

The first serious attempt to use electronic books for serious literary pursuit came with Adobe's Portable Document Format or PDF. Since PDF is the format digital printers use this is also the most widely used format in the Internet today. PDF is excellent for designing nice colored documents with charts and images where the layout is important.

On the negative side, PDF is a rigid, inflexible format, according to some it is pretty bad for reading novels. The reader can not easily change the font size or style to match their preferences.

EPUB is an open industry ebook format. This is the format that Apple, Barnes&Noble, Sony, Kobo, Diesel e-Book, and others use. If your book is available in EPUB, it can be read on the most popular e-book readers and ebook reading software applications (Like Stanza on the iPhone or Aldiko on Android devices), and will gain the widest readership outside of Amazon. Barnes&Noble also started to sell the Nook, the electronic reading device that is supposed to compete with the Amazon's Kindle.

Mobipocket (Kindle) –Mobipocket, A.K.A. MOBI, facilitates your books to be read on the Amazon Kindle, since Amazon is far the biggest online book seller, and e-Book are for online market; this format is extremely important. Mobipocket is also supported on many handheld devices and e-reading applications, there is even a free PC application that lets you buy books on the Kindle to be read it on your laptop.

These two major formats (and there are more) locked in a deadly conflict, vying for supremacy of the electronic publishing market; this maybe reminding some of you the "wars" of eight track tape versus the cassette or the battle of DVD-RAM versus the DVD+RW. Do not be overly concerned with this. As a writer or content provider, you just make sure your book is well crafted and available for both the Kindle and the Nook.

I use two software packages one of is a paid software to e-book formatting and creation. First I must make sure that the manuscript is in open office .odt format, with the chapter titles styled as heading. Then I start Anthemion Jutoh[8] software to create the EPUB format. At this point you should also have a e-book cover. The software is excellent and even errors are intuitively solved by the software (most of the time).

The other, free software I use is Calibre[9] to catalogue and convert my e-book. Often I find and e-book to print and with Calibre I can convert the EPUB to .rtf thus make it readable to Open Office or MS Word.

Interestingly, I no longer own MS Word.

What is DRM?

Digital Rights Management encrypts your eBook so it cannot be decompiled or read on another device. In other words, it protects it like a lock. The Nook and B&N applications can read it, so if a customer purchased a DRM eBook and they're logged into their device or application on their computer, they can read the (their)

---

8   Jutoh is a eBook authoring tool from Anthemion Software. It can create e-Book in EPUB and other formats compatible with popular eBook stores like Amazon Kindle and Apple iBooks. Jutoh can be used to quickly create e-Book by importing formatted documents. It can also be used by advanced users to create e-Book..

9   Calibre is an eBook manager, organizer and reader with which you will have an organized and cataloged collection, on top of having the possibility to adapt the files to the reader format that you need according to your device. You will be able to organize your collection on author, publication date or publisher among others.

eBook. Since the breaking of DRM is now on equal footing with breaking of spreadsheet or Adobe Pdf passwords, I recommend against using this. It won 't protect your creation but could possibly alienate a potential purchases.

There is a lot of information available online about eBook formatting but much of it is either outdated or plain wrong. Apple now demands the latest ePub format, which is 1.0.5. In order to comply with this you would need to use a software called PDFto-ePub created by

Dongsoft (http://www.pdf-epub-converter.com/). It is advisable that you, through your publishing company, participate in the electronic publishing revolution as a content provider. It is usually free and your book can be uploaded and live on the Internet as digital content in a matter of hours. (During the production of this book Amazon made this process a little longer and it no longer accepts just any public domain content into its digital library. The submission must be unique to be accepted.)

Not all of your books should be on the Internet as an e-book. Use your judgment and business sense. You will never see the book you are reading on it. It is tempting but I am greedy. Any how-to book that contains have mission critical and unique information as content should not be on Kindle.

I rather send this book in print for a number of reviewers and industry experts for free than make paltry sum for myself but enrich Amazon's coffers using the Kindle.

If you thought from reading this book that 55-percent discount is bad than how would you feel about 65-percent? I am appalled by 65-percent and hope that you are too, which is precisely the discount Amazon requires their publishers to settle for. You can often see public domain books offered for free or for 1 dollar.

Barnes and Noble and Apple's iBookstore are both better for the public domain titles. The Book for Barnes and Noble offers better terms for content providers. For books selling between $2.99 and $9.99 the Barnes and Noble offers better terms for content providers. For books selling between $2.99 and $9.99 the percent royalty. ((B&N press[10]) Publishers will be paid a royalty off the List Price according to the following terms: For e-book with a List Price at or between $2.99 and $9.99 65% of the List Price For e-book with a List Price at or below $2.98 or at or greater than $10.00 (but not more than $199.99 and not less than $0.99) 40% of the List Price)

E -book publishing might be worth the effort, even if you have created something new, fresh and popular. I have over a hundred some titles on Kindle and my profit margin now is better than

10   Formerly know as Pubit

printed books. Even when you mark your own book as 20-percent discount with LSI, it is not always advisable to do so for public domain titles.

After the housing crash e-books were amazingly popular and risk free and this is why you can introduce your book and set a promotional price in hoping that some people will buy the printed version as well.

At the time of writing this book it has been noted that sales of e-books plunged 17% in the U.K. in 2016, according to the Publishers Association. Sales of physical books and journals went up by 7% over the same period, while children's books surged 16%.

The same trend is on display in the U.S., where e-book sales declined 18.7% over the first nine months of 2016, according to the Association of American Publishers. Paperback sales were up 7.5% over the same period, and hardback sales increased 4.1%.

Lightning Source has contracted with a number of businesses to provide content to a Print on Demand machine called The Espresso Book Machine®. The Espresso Book Machine (EBM) is a print on demand (POD) machine that prints, collates, covers, and binds a single book in a few minutes. A single machine can cost approximately $175,000. You as a LSI customer can provide content for this new sales channel by signing additional contract addendum.

Google Book Search

Book Search begun as internet giant Google decided on an ambitious, new effort to catalog, digitize every book in print available online. Since the inception of this program it has been mired with controversy and a class action suit from authors and publishers. Despite this controversy every book listed with Lulu.com is still available to be submitted to the Book Search program. Once the book is part of the Google catalog, links and comparative pricing information are provided on how to purchase the printed copy.

Since Google had settled with the plaintiffs over copyright issues it is now free and well positioned to enter the potentially lucrative eBook sales. Since the company has entered the smartphone business, taking on the iPhone and it has decided to offer content on these devices. At the writing of this chapter Google is the laggard on the electronic publishing and sales, quite a distance behind Amazon, Apple and Barnes and Noble. Google however will not accept public domain books.

XIV. Using AI

All print-on-demand publishers will ask if your content was used using artificial intelligence (AI).

AI is an uncharted territory for all aspects of business and personal life. Translators, Editors and many other professionals are afraid that AI would replace them in the workforce. These fears are not unfounded. Amazon KDP, and Ingram both implemented a new policy regarding AI.

Any editing, writing, or translating using AI must be disclosed. Proper execution allows the content to stay published.

It is, of course, tempting to rewrite public domain works using AI and copyright them as your own; or imitate an author and claim that AI published content as hers. This is what happened on Amazon when In August 2023, Jane Friedman, the author, expressed her dissatisfaction over several books, mislabeled as her creations by AI tools. Amazon subsequently removed the books.

There is an AI editing, translating and content creating software called Quillbot.

The Software started out as a paraphrasing tool and for what it does it is very affordable.

But that's not all.
Quillbot is proud to offer the following features:

- The tool for paraphrasing
- English grammar checker
- Translator
- Ensuring originality
- The integration of all other tools is the responsibility of the co-writer.
- A summarizer
- Formulating citations

A trio of individuals—Anil Jason, Rohit Gupta, and David Silin created QuillBot in 2017. Since then, it has steadily added new features and taken off as a powerful tool, with large user base.

XV. My Ten Commandments

This book is a guideline for a hands-off, part-time business that can grow into whatever you inspire it to be. If you love doing this business as much as I do, then there is no doubt in my mind that you will succeed. This is a key ingredient: a passion for what you do. On the other hand, if you only do this for the money, slacking interest in the literary world, your path will be harder and a little more arduous.

No "bible" can be without its Ten Commandments. These are my ten basic rules for public domain publishing.

1. Be selective with your public domain content. There are literally hundreds of thousands of books out there, but not every one of them should be republished.

2. Be creative and professional in your modifications and alterations of public domain content. Use an illustrator or a ghost writer if you must. Over the long run, it will be well worth it.

3. I try to limit my business to wholesale only because I value my time, and sales tax in California, where I live, is a hassle to collect. My time is worth more.

4. When republishing just about anything, you should work with Lightning Source; you should not use Amazon KDP. While KDP yields guaranteed Amazon listings, they can arbitrarily close you down.

5. Try to do as much of the setup and design phases of your book business as possible. You will save money, and you may even fall in love with some of the creative aspects.

6. Use reasonable free-lancers judiciously to leverage yourself and manage tasks that you cannot yet do. 7. Take a long-term view! As with any business, this is not a 100-yard sprint but a Boston marathon. Short-term views can often beget shortsighted views.

8. Learn to work with Amazon.com and LSI effectively. They can make or break your business. 9. Try to work with independent

bookstores around the English-speaking world. It takes some effort, but it will pay off.

10. Write about what you know. You have built a publishing business, and now you can be published as well. Many people spend a lifetime in vain just to do that.

Appendix A: Public Domain Resources

Expired copyrights can be searched for books published after 1978 at.
https://cocatalog.loc.gov

Project Gutenberg
http://www.gutenberg.org/catalog/
This is the oldest if not the largest volunteer effort to digitize and archive cultural works. It was founded in 1971 by Michael S. Hart.

University of Pennsylvania's Online Books Page http://online-Book.library.upenn.edu/ The Online Books Page was founded, and is edited, by John Mark Ockerbloom; He is a digital library planner and researcher at the University of Pennsylvania.

The Internet Sacred Text Archive http://www.sacred-texts.com/ This is a collection of electronic texts about religion, mythology, legends and folklore, and occult and esoteric topics. Texts are presented in English translation and, where possible, in the original language.

Bartleby
http://www.bartleby.com/
This is an old web site of classic, public domain books; the format of books sometimes overlaps the project Gutenberg's but the html format is easier to use. Knowledge Rush
http://www.knowledgerush.com/kr/jsp/db/directory.jsp
100 Great Books in the Public Domain
The Digital Book Index
http://www.digitalbookindex.org/about.htm Digital Book Index provides links to more than 145,000 full-text digital books from more than 1800 commercial and non-commercial publishers, universities, and various private sites. More than 100,000 of these books, texts, and documents are available free.

The sites below primarily provide search engines, indexes or useful link lists for finding online books.
ATHENA (multilingual text index in Switzerland)
http://un2sg4.unige.ch/athena/html/athome.html
Digital Book Index (free and for-pay books online; registration-based) http://www.digitalbookindex.com/
E-Books on the Web (multi-index search engine from Buffalo) http://libweb.lib.buffalo.edu/ft/E-Book.html
Internet Public Library Online Texts (an index of sites) http://

www.ipl.org/div/subject/browse/hum60.60.00/

OAISter (search for lots of digital library resources, text and otherwise) http://oaister.umdl.umich.edu/o/oaister/

Samizdat Express (eclectic collection of texts and pointers) http://www.samizdat.com/

Voice of the Shuttle and its English Literature section http://vos.ucsb.edu/

Everything else we see worth listing that doesn't fit in more specialized categories.

The EServer (over 30,000 texts, though many are short) http://eserver.org/

UVA Digital Text Collections and its modern English collection (about 5,000 publicly available texts) http://www.lib.virginia.edu/digital/collections/text/

Humanities Text Initiative (at UMichigan) http://www.hti.umich.edu/

Universal Digital Library Repository (million book collection; quality highly variable) http://www.ulib.org/

University of Toronto Books Online (800+ titles as page images) http://link.library.utoronto.ca/booksonline/index.cfm

Wiretap Electronic Text Archive (one of the oldest etext collections still online) http://wiretap.area.com/

Oxford Text Archive (in the UK) http://ota.ox.ac.uk/

The Bibliomania Library (from Data Text) http://www.bibliomania.com/

Book Glutton (annotates and chat about 1000+ books as you read them) http://www.bookglutton.com/

Eldritch Press (books with annotations and illustrations) http://www.eldritchpress.org/

University of Toronto English Library http://www.library.utoronto.ca/utel/ PSU Electronic Classics (PDF versions of classic texts) http://www2.hn.psu.edu/faculty/jmanis/jimspdf.htm

Electronic Open Stacks (preservation digitization at Chicago) http://www.lib.uchicago.edu/e/ets/eos/

National Library of Canada Electronic Collection (archives texts from or about Canada) http://collection.nlc-bnc.ca/e-coll-e/index-e.htm

E-Book@Adelaide (1000+ HTML editions of classic and Australia-related literature)
http://etext.library.adelaide.edu.au/
Digital Books in the KSL Collection (400+ digitized titles on various subjects)
http://library.case.edu/digitalcase/BrowseObjects.aspx?PID=ksl:digitalb ooksCollection
IntraText Digital Library (5000+ texts, multilingual, main focus on religion, Latin, Italian, and science)
http://www.intratext.com/

Photographs
Public domain images, royalty free stock photos http://www.public-domain-image.com/
Free Public Domain Database http://www.pdphoto.org/
USDA ARS Image Gallery
http://www.ars.usda.gov/is/graphics/photos/
USGA Photographic Library
http://libraryphoto.cr.usgs.gov/
Library of Congress Prints and Photographs Reading Room http://lcweb.loc.gov/rr/print
United States Antarctic Program http://photolibrary.usap.gov/
Library of Congress Public Domain Reprint Service http://lcweb.loc.gov/preserv/pds
The George Eastman House International Museum http://www.eastmanhouse.org/
New York Public Library Photo Collection
http://www.nypl.org/research/chss/spe/art/photo/photo.html
National Archives and Records
http://www.archives.gov/research/arc/

Public Domain Pictures
http://www.princetonol.com/groups/iad/links/clipart.html
Wikipedia
http://en.wikipedia.org/wiki/Public_domain_image_resources
Maps
The University of Minnesota Links to Map Libraries http://map.lib.umn.edu
Oddens' Bookmarks
http://oddens.georg.uu.nl/main.html
Geography and Map Division of the Library of Congress http://www.loc.gov/rr/geogmap/gmpage.html

www.ingramcontent.com/pod-product-compliance
Lightning Source LLC
Chambersburg PA
CBHW060139050426
42448CB00010B/2201